THE ENGAGEMENT HABIT

For **the People** who are **Screaming on the Inside**

Mark Gregory and **Alex** Lewis

First paperback edition March 2021

Book design by Definition Consulting
Cover photography & internal illustrations © Shutterstock.com

ISBN 978-1-8384202-0-8

Contents

Foreword

I was delighted to be asked to write the foreword to this important new book from Alex and Mark. Based on their extensive personal experience, it sets out clearly why a workplace culture of engaging employees both in their organisational purpose and in their day to day work, produces such positive results for both the organisation and the individual. Equally importantly and convincingly, in clear and coherent steps, it sets out how leaders and managers can set out and advance on the engagement journey.

I first met them more than a decade ago, following the publication of the Engaging for Success report I co-authored with my friend David Macleod, when both were working in aircraft production for BAE Systems at Warton and Samlesbury in the north-west.

> Their work there literally revolutionised performance in an industry of vital importance to our country

Their work there literally revolutionised performance in an industry of vital importance to our country; by gaining the trust of employees, they succeeded in transforming the culture from command and control to front line empowerment, enabling modernisation of working practices, and taking the trade unions – fearful that such change would be the thin end of the deskilling wedge for individuals – along on the journey. And their enthusiasm and approach was embraced across the company, including by the then Chief Executive.

It was truly a culture change programme ahead of its time, and I can genuinely say it was an inspiration to me, demonstrating as it did that 'this employee engagement thing' really does work!

Over the years both have been generous with their time in supporting the government sponsored Engage for Success movement which arose out of our report; Alex was an indefatigable asset, taking the engagement message out far and wide as a member of our task force. And Mark bought a detailed understanding of how some of our 'big picture' enthusiasms could be enacted on the ground, in individual workplaces, through front line empowerment techniques and strategies that enabled employees to solve problems, use their expertise, and bring their best selves to work.

As they say in the book, while a decade ago 'people stuff' was considered soft and fluffy and consigned to human resources, these days employee engagement does feature in the boardroom, not least as a result of the Financial Reporting Council's revised Corporate Governance Code which requires companies to report on employee matters. But many organisations, while getting to grips with the 'why', are having real difficulty with the 'how'.

Changing the culture - the 'how we do things around here' – to one where people are enabled to collaborate, to innovate, and live all those values which we see on the laminated posters on the wall and on the mouse mats, is hard. To build trust- the essential magic ingredient on engagement – means behaviours which bring the values to life, behaviours which are lived every day, by everyone in the organisation, without exception, which are non-negotiable.

And that is where this book comes in. Not only is it a guide to the steps organisations can take, it also explains why these steps matter; there may be no short cuts, but there is a road map. It de-mystifies some of the impenetrable jargon that inevitably accrues around 'people management' topics. It is a must-read for CEOs, for HR and communications staff, and for leaders and managers in the line.

I really admire these two. They have been steadfast in their belief in the importance of engagement, and in taking that message out. They are true evangelists for people at work. I hope we can continue to work together, united in the belief that 'it's the people, stupid!' More power to their collective elbows!

Nita Clarke OBE
Director IPA
Co-founder Engage for Success

I really admire these two. They have been steadfast in their belief in the importance of engagement, and in taking that message out. They are true evangelists for people at work. I hope we can continue to work together, united in the belief that 'it's the people, stupid!' More power to their collective elbows!

Mark Gregory

Mark Gregory left school at sixteen and started work within a small family run engineering business. Having completed a technical apprenticeship, he went on to study for a degree in Mechanical & Manufacturing Engineering (BEng), followed by an MSc in Engineering Management.

Post University, Mark joined Toyota Motor Manufacturing (UK) Ltd where he was a manufacturing engineer for ten years, in both the UK and Japan. He went on to work in operations management roles for Ford Motor Company across Europe for seven years, before exchanging cars for planes to work in various large operational senior leadership roles for BAE Systems Ltd, where he spent eight years.

During his career, Mark has held a belief that all benefits in business stem from having engaged employees, and he never understood why other leaders and the organisation didn't. In 2012, he founded his own company, Unleash & Engage, of which he is currently Managing Director.

Alex Lewis

Alex Lewis graduated with an Industrial Studies degree from London University, before joining Siemens, where he worked in HR management roles, in the UK and Germany. He then spent two years with EDS, a Hewlett Packard company, followed by seven years with Airbus and then ten years with BAE Systems.

In his time with BAE Systems he was HR Director in both the air and maritime divisions, where he managed twenty thousand people, as well as Director of employee relations and engagement. Alex was a founder member of the UK Government Employee Engagement Taskforce.

During his corporate career, Alex worked hard to get businesses to see that engaged employees were the key to sustainable business results and the way to engage them was not just from the corporate centre out, but also by real people doing real work. Alex is now a Director of Unleash & Engage.

> Mark and Alex spent a lot of their career screaming on the inside!

It's not about *planning.*

Engagement is a participation sport.

Remember, **no one** got fit by *planning* to go to the gym.

How to use this book

Throughout the authors' time in leadership roles, Mark and Alex grasped the importance of involving and engaging their teams. This was born out of instinct, as opposed to education. Much of their shared experience with the Engage for Success Taskforce, felt like a job of trying to codify common sense. Whilst many leaders understand that creating engagement is something they should automatically do; how to do it, remains something of a mystery. This book aims to solve that mystery.

The ultimate purpose of this book is to convey practical insights, drawn from the authors' in-depth employee engagement experience, in both their corporate and consulting careers.

Who It's For

This book has a key message for three specific groups:

The Business Leader

The business leader: the chief executive officer, director or owner, who believes in the importance of their staff having a personal preference and being treated as they would wish to be treated themselves, but who struggles with the formidable task of creating a team culture. Whether your team is comprised of 50, 500 or 500,000 members, creating a culture can feel impossible. Alternatively, they may quite simply not have a clue what to do.

The Corporate Centre

The corporate centre ("Centre of Excellence") or an HR Leader who receives direct instruction from the business leader to create the culture, or they assume it is their role to create the culture.

The People Manager

The people manager who builds the culture within their team.

We would hope that everyone who picks up this book is inspired to read it cover to cover. However, we also recognise that life is busy for us all, so we want to be clear on the essentials. If you're the CEO, sorry there is no short cut, we recommend you read all chapters of this book.

The best route for a CEO to create the culture they want is to role model the desired habits and behaviours. Or in Gandhi's words, **"be the change you want to see in the world"**. Create an expectation for others to do the same. If you're in the corporate centre or an HR Leader, you'll find the essential information you need is in chapters two and four. The recommended route for you is to coach those in the line and support those who cast the greatest shadow across their organisations. If you're a People Manager who wants to unleash the power of your team, the key points for you are in chapters two, five and six. People Managers need to know that culture is created by consistent habits, and by practicing those habits with intensity and frequency. Frequency means practicing the habits regularly so that they become the norm, intensity means practicing them with full commitment and belief.

Whatever your particular role, once you figure out which habits will work for your situation, I urge you not to delay. Jump in and just get on with it.

> "Be the change you want to see in the world"
>
> Gandhi

Hundreds of small **habit changes** led to a gradual **yet dramatic**

change in the conversation.

So What Is This Engagement Thing?

> We are what we repeatedly do. Excellence, then, is not an act but a habit.
>
> Aristotle

It would be traditional to start with an academic definition of what engagement is. Let's not do that.

Instead, let's begin with a story from Mark's early career:

The Tom and Paul Story

At age sixteen, whilst still at school, although not achieving great academic heights, Mark found a job in a local engineering firm. Mark was about to encounter his first exposure to employee engagement, and in hindsight, he wishes that he knew then, what he knows now.

Glaswegian Tom was his supervisor. He was an ex-parachute regiment sergeant who was quite as formidable as you might expect. He only had one 'motivational' technique, which was to continually tear strips off people. As his irritation deepened throughout the day, Tom would gradually turn a bright shade of red, from the neck up. The angrier he grew, the more potent his Glaswegian accent. He would burst onto the scene, ranting, but Mark and his co-workers didn't understand a word. After Tom exited the shop floor in disgust, they would look at each other, to see if anybody had managed to decipher what he had been trying to tell them.

Nobody did, and invariably, Tom would reappear fifteen minutes later for yet another rant-filled attempt at forcing the troops into line. On Mark's first day on the job, Tom led him out onto the shop floor and explained that there were only three tools he would need. Tom proudly presented Mark with a broom, a shovel, and a wheelbarrow. Mark still remembers Tom's exact words, **'Your job is to shovel shit.'** Tom then proceeded to drill Mark, to check that he fully understood his assignment. At a loss to know what to say, Mark agreed that his job was to shovel shit! And that's how his career in manufacturing commenced.

After two weeks of shovelling, Mark noticed a pattern: a pile of metal chippings kept appearing in the same spot, next to a metal cutting components machine. After careful observation, he realised that metal filings spilt from the guarding of the machine, to form a heap on the floor. Hence, the pile which repeatedly presented itself for Mark to remove.

Wanting to be useful, Mark decided to solve the problem so he wouldn't have to keep wasting his time shovelling. Suitably proud of his innovative ideas, Mark dashed off to relay the good news to Tom. Mark had barely begun when Tom roared, 'What's your job?' 'To shovel shit,' Mark spluttered, enthusiasm instantly quashed. **Tom told Mark in no uncertain terms, that he must get on with his job and stop coming to him with fancy ideas.**

After another couple of weeks of removing the daily pile, Mark's natural enthusiasm resurfaced, and he began to wonder whether he might have simply caught Tom on an off-day. Why wouldn't he want to solve the problem? Not easily deterred, Mark worked up the courage to approach Tom once more, to broach the pile topic. Tom extended his palm towards Mark's face and shouted at him to stop bothering him with this nonsense.

As Mark turned to flee, one of the old guys on the team put his arm around Mark's shoulders and told

Tom was management, and **management just didn't care.**

him that he knew he meant well, but it was pointless. Tom was management, and management just didn't care. So, for the next nine months, Mark kept his young head down, his gob shut and did exactly as he had been ordered.

Fortunately, Tom retired, and a new supervisor called Paul took his place. One morning, Paul asked for a few minutes of Mark's time. He led him into the canteen, they grabbed a cup of tea and sat down. Paul asked Mark how old he was. He was taken aback because he was certain Paul knew the answer to his question.

Mark replied that he was seventeen, and Paul asked whether he wanted to be shovelling dirt for the rest of his days. When Mark assured him that he didn't, Paul asked what he wanted to do with his life. That day, Paul opened the door to Mark's future; he offered him an opportunity to better himself. Immediately, his mind jumped to the design office; Mark sensed that was the ideal job for him. Paul challenged Mark to show him what he was capable of and then promised to see what could be done. Mark needed no further encouragement. Where Tom had dismissed his ideas, Paul took the time to avidly listen. Three months later Mark became an office junior.

The point of this story is that there are Toms and Pauls in every business. If Toms are at one extreme, and Pauls at the other, most leaders fall somewhere in-between on the Tom-Paul spectrum.

This was Mark's first exposure to employee engagement, and it sparked a huge shift in his world. If not for Paul, Mark may never have got his break. Mark and I explain how to understand a leader's position on the Tom-Paul spectrum. And the content of this book is designed to move you closer to the Paul example. I'm guessing you have a similar story of your own. The sad truth is that most of us have several 'Tom' stories, but only one or two experiences which feature a 'Paul'.

The challenge for all of us who want the workplace to be more productive, more stimulating, and more fun, is to **be a Paul, <u>not</u> a Tom**: to develop organisations of Pauls and create an environment where future Pauls can flourish. The reality is, we all know what engagement is when we experience it. Mark and I, both entered the world of work in the late 1980s, a time when the typical image of a motivated workforce was measured by the number of days lost in strike action and on any individual level by how enthusiastically you involved yourself in the absence rota. Amidst the shoulder pads and perms, bosses had no conception that sharing company strategy would be worthwhile. At best, the assumption would be that workers would be disinterested, at worst, that any suggestion of opportunity would just be seen as an act of selfish defiance and the opportunity to attempt to make a baseline for higher pay demands.

In contrast to Mark's experience with Tom and Paul, I spent a decade in HR director roles, one of which was a central role as employee relations and engagement director for one of the world's largest engineering companies. Alongside colleagues, in similar size companies, I worked for a board with a keen desire to improve engagement in their organisation. Engagement had become a topic of conversation in Harvard business review, amongst the IOD (Institute of Directors) and the CBI (Confederation of British Industry). It had become fashionable in C-Suite circles. I remember a rather sheepish board member, immediately before a board meeting, asking me what this engagement thing was all about! I tried to explain in my best Queen's English. The board member in question scribbled notes, thanked me and then spent the hour discussing employee engagement whilst nodding furiously. I was convinced he had no idea what I was talking about, and even less idea what to actually do.

What followed, for many, in similar roles across the industry, was a request for a monthly engagement strategy: a Gantt chart, with an accompanying silver bullet that would presumably, provide an instant translation. Money was put aside for increasing the spend on the employee survey; surely this was the place where the action plan would emerge?

In reality, things only started to change as a result of leaders in the global business, following the lead of the CEO. Ultimately, people follow what you do, not what you say. The small but significant habit changes instigated by CEOs and Divisional MDs were quickly replicated by senior managers who began to model the behaviours.

"This is just what we do around here", became

the new normal. More time was spent visiting and listening to employees, as opposed to reviewing PowerPoint presentations. Blogs appeared, demonstrating the human side of leaders, rather than instructional briefing posters. Hundreds of small habit changes led to a gradual yet dramatic change in the conversation. The outcome was increased levels of trust, clarity, and yes, improved engagement scores!

Engagement Beliefs

In 2011 I was honoured to be invited to take part in a government task force, alongside David MacLeod and Nita Clarke, and about twenty of my counterparts from UK companies: from private, public, and the third sector.

Our brief was simple: Operationalise a report written by David and Nita, Engaging for Success: enhancing performance through employee engagement, which had been sponsored by the previous labour government.

Over the next two years, we established materials to help people understand how employee engagement works. We formed a coalition of chief executives and company chairmen in the UK, to support the goal, created a framework to describe what engagement looks like, and developed guidance on a variety of topics. I led a group on how to effectively engage in times of restructuring. We did some great work, and undoubtedly, **we helped to change the conversation that took place in the UK.** However, all these years on, and there's still a gap in terms of the practical tips and the application, to help People Managers to effectively create employee engagement.

In this book, we deliberately avoid complex models and frameworks, instead focusing on the practical. However, our work is underpinned by the following four beliefs:

Belief 1 People Protect What They Build.

What this means is, don't tell people how to do things, tell them what needs to be done, and encourage them to work out how to do it for themselves. If they build the solution, it will be theirs and they will protect it and adapt it because they are engaged in it.

Belief 2 Culture is just a collection of habits.

All habitual behaviour forms a loop which starts with a cue (the stimulus), contains a routine (the pattern of behaviour and activity) and a reward (which motivates you to repeat the routine). Habits can be engineered by understanding the current situation through thoughtful design of the cue, the routine and the reward. In organisations, we talk about culture without really knowing what it is - culture is the sum of those habits.

Belief 3 Habits are built through intensity and frequency.

Making anything habitual requires intensity (genuine commitment) and frequency (repetition). When starting to practice a new habit, it will feel awkward at first (try brushing your teeth with the wrong hand and tell me how that feels!), but over time the practice becomes second-nature.

Belief 4 People copy what you do, not what you say.

In our work, we describe this as the shadow of the leader. Leaders role model certain habits, and as a result of genetic and social conditioning this becomes the norm. People do not copy what you say, particularly if you then do the opposite.

We won't spend time trying to convince you there is a case for engagement. If you don't believe that an engaged team will give you better outcomes and a better workplace in which to spend your time, you're reading the wrong book!

In Engaging for Success, Nita Clarke liked to joke that one day she would create a website called, 'Work doesn't have to be shit.com'. I have worked with highly engaged teams and had wonderful

> Work doesn't have to be shit.com
>
> Nita Clarke

experiences which I still remember vividly. Work can be enjoyable for people and we all deserve that!

Between us, Mark and I have facilitated high engagement in some extremely tough and varied environments, such as steelwork, shipyards and service environments. As a result, these companies have become highly engaged, with impressive safety benchmarks across their industry, leaders in productivity, and the type of organisations, any leader would be proud to lead.

Fast-forward thirty years from the days when most leaders barely knew what the term "employee engagement" meant, and nowadays, even the most aggressive of company bosses would accept that a motivated workforce is an essential aspiration. And in most boardrooms, the topic of employee engagement is now an open discussion.

However, there is still an abstract alien concept to the **"Employee Engagement" discussion**: as if employees aren't human beings who just want to live their best life.

Mark and I have observed that posturing, planning and endless talk, rarely lead to a coherent plan.

Ultimately, as the title of the book indicates, this is for those who are 'screaming on the inside'. We feel we spent much of our careers bemused and frustrated as to why those around us did not get it. Surely, involving people in your team and looking to help them be their best self is just common sense? Instead, we observed a continual treadmill of centrally driven engagement initiatives that drained the life out of the organisation and the people.

We desperately hope that the world of work is not still full of people having to build business cases and convince others of the need for engagement, but sadly, though our consulting work we see that there is still a fair amount of the workforce at every level, screaming on the inside when anyone mentions the Engagement word. Suppose you are a CEO, a specialist or an ambitious People Manager. In that case, we hope that some of the practical thoughts in this book help you to find the courage, the language and the skills to take back control of your engagement opportunity and quite simply, make your place of work a better place to be. Your team deserve it, and so do you!

Engagement is a fundamental necessity that drives transformation throughout your organisation, so I urge you to stop talking and instead start building the new habits we will share with you in this book.

Engagement is a **fundamental necessity**

that drives transformation throughout your organisation.

The Foundations of Engagement: Habits and Trust.

Warning:

First, we must cover a bit of theory, but I will make it as enjoyable as possible. . .

To build high engagement, I've discovered there are two fundamental principles you must accept.

The first is that **Engagement is a set of habits**, and the second is that **Trust is at the root of every relationship.**

If you don't accept these principles, you can try to build engagement by following the advice in this book, but be warned; it will feel as though you're pushing water uphill with a fork.

Therefore, I recommend, you spend some time absorbing the content in this chapter and use it as the foundation upon which to build your plans. Fortunately, these principles apply to numerous areas of life and work, so you'll be rewarded exponentially for your efforts.

Every organisation that I've consulted with and worked in was trying to change something for the better. I've found that there is often a scale of organisation, focus and delivery around the change agenda, where at one extreme there is an army of people, teams, external consultants, war rooms, scheduled reviews, programme and project managers, change KPI's, and a cadence of review and reporting. And on the other, there is a lot of leadership talk, but no action. It's been my experience that it doesn't really matter where your organisation is on this scale because this isn't how change occurs. Nothing is ever changed purely by PowerPoint, theoretical models or well-intentioned discussions. Change only occurs by working with real people doing real work.

When people want better engagement, what they're saying is that they desire change, and what that translates to at the most fundamental level is that their business currently has a set of habits that aren't working, and they need to adopt a new set of habits. As the holders of the habits are people; no presentation, model or KPI reporting will ever work in isolation. What you've got to do is to connect with the people who are discharging the activities within the business, and help them to change their habits. Put another way - to turn our four beliefs into actuality. We should never forget that a company is simply a collection of people.

When they discharge their duties, the business forms a set of habits, some of which duplicate throughout the business with everyone operating the same way, while some habits are unique to individuals.

The adage that we're creatures of habit is true. Culture is essentially just a collection of habits.

For example, if you have a 'safety culture' you will find that people do things like wearing the appropriate Personal Protective Equipment (PPE) on a habitual basis. If you have high levels of trust from your customers you will generally find that people in your organisation do what they say they will do, and it is habitual. I hear people in organisations talk about culture a lot as if it is some sort of black-box concept, but culture is really simple; it is just a collection of the habitual routines that people perform, generally, unconsciously.

The other thing that's important in the engagement proposition when you talk about change is the reality that most businesses not only struggle to change, but they also struggle to maintain the change. **There are many more change initiatives dead in the water than there are successful transformations, and the reason for this is the only way you sustain change is when it becomes habitual.** If it's not internalised to the point at which it becomes habitual, people soon revert to their old ways because old habits continue to exist alongside the new ones.

In the worst-case scenario, old habits dominate because people are more comfortable with the familiar, and so the exciting initiatives fizzle out along with the new habits.

Habits are critical for sustainment, and our ability to sustain engagement is a result of an individual's engagement habits, particularly those of organisational role models, such as People Managers.

> I believe leaders are not always people in authority because leadership is influence based. Subsequently, the leader is whoever we choose to follow, and isn't necessarily the boss.

It's worth noting that I don't hold a traditional view of leaders: I believe leaders are not always people in authority because leadership is influence based. Subsequently, the leader is whoever we choose to follow, and isn't necessarily the boss.

In this book, we frequently use the term **'shadow of the leader'**, by which we mean: role modelling, which is about what people see you do habitually and then they choose to follow.

Whatever is consistently role modelled, implicitly transmits an unspoken message to people, which implies a standard of acceptable behaviour. Just like children, adults tend to do what we do, not what we say they should do; whether we like it or not.

The study of Habits forms a new body of research in comparison to other more established areas of Neuroscience. You can find extensive studies, papers and books on the subject of habits, but for this book, I want to keep it simple. I want you to think of a habit as a pathway in your brain that takes you from A to B via a defined route.

Therefore, to achieve the desired change or transformation, what you're essentially saying is, 'I used to go from A to B via a defined route, and now I want to go from A to B or A to C via a new route, and to do that, I need to develop a new habit'.

When you create a new habit, you build a new pathway. The more you walk the same path, the smoother it becomes until eventually there is a clear and distinct track to follow (in your mind), which becomes natural, effortless, and more beneficial than trying to go back down the old route.

When you create a new habit, **you build a new pathway.**

When we consult with organisations, we give people the analogy that a current habit is like a three-lane motorway. In contrast, forming a new, desirable habit is like hacking through the jungle.

The more you travel along the path, the smoother it becomes until one day it supersedes the old three lane motorway, and now you have an easy and familiar route.

Only at this point does the new habit replace the existing habit, and this is why it can be challenging to establish new habits; you're hacking through the jungle, instead of speeding down a smooth three-lane motorway. The previous pathway to the destination; the old habit, doesn't disappear, but just becomes an unused, overgrown pathway.

An excellent example is that of why you can still ride a bike when you haven't ridden one for years, and this is because the 'riding a bike pathway' still exists in your brain. The saying, 'It's like riding a bike', illustrates this perfectly. You might be a bit wobbly on the bike at first, but the original neural pathway still exists, and so it's far more natural to re-establish than to create a completely new route. If you then ride the bike every day, it will soon become a three-lane motorway again.

People struggle to ditch old, familiar habits because the neural pathways don't disappear even when the paths are overgrown, which is why alcoholics have a strong tendency to resume their alcoholism when they're not vigilant; otherwise known as 'falling off the wagon'. Likewise, someone who has struggled with their weight for an extended period is likely at some point to be tempted down the old pathway and to eat too many bars of chocolate, or whatever food they love. If the guilty pleasure or reward of the old habit outweigh the benefits of the new behaviour, they're more likely to revert to the old way of eating. The new behaviour isn't yet an established habit, which is why weight loss programmes rarely work long term for people.

A good example of an overgrown pathway is when you are only able to recall snippets of things which you know you fully understood in your youth, such as when you're helping your kids with their homework. Typically, as soon as you read the textbook, it triggers the memory of how it works because the neural pathway still exists.

Building the Engagement Habit

People often ask me what it takes to start building the engagement Habit. There are three necessary elements.

The first is Knowledge: It's essential to be aware of why you should engage in the first place. As you're reading this book, you're already interested and trying to figure it out, with or without the help of your organisation.

For me, it was a collision of events: it was the combination of remembering what it was like and having the desire to be at the Paul end of the spectrum as a leader and the fact that the business I was leading had plateaued in performance along with my career. This set of circumstances sparked my interest and action into learning about engagement, but everyone must find their reason why, or their efforts will soon fizzle out.

The second is Skill: How do you engage? That's what the remainder of the chapters in this book cover, as well as providing insight into how to create and sustain new habits.

The third is Attitude: The desire to engage, build the habits and keep deploying those engagement habits minute by minute, day by day, week by week... While you can get help to do this from other people, ultimately this is down to you.

Building Habits that Stick

In my experience, there is a recipe for building strong habits, and like all good recipes, there are some key ingredients. The first three are commonly known as The Habit Loop. To build any habit, you need a Cue, which serves as a trigger that tells your brain to go and use the Habit.

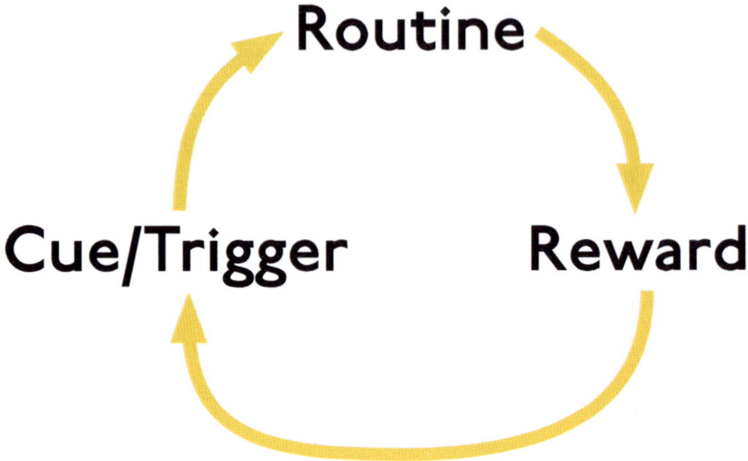

You also need a routine (remember the route from A to B), so this is the routine you follow and maybe physical, mental or emotional. And the third is the Reward: remember the guilty pleasure; the thing that makes you want to do it all over again, which is typically a specific result or a dopamine rush? The Cue, Routine and Reward are all essential for a habit to stick.

The fourth thing you need to understand to build a habit is the awareness of what might be holding you back from building the new habit in the first place, or what I call 'The Current Paradigm'. A paradigm is just the way you view something today; it is not good or bad; it is simply a view. But this view can stop you from building a new habit in the first place, and interrupt your efforts. Think about what would stop you, or what is stopping you from initiating the habit loop. It could be as simple as you don't believe it will work or you don't think you have time. It is useful to think about what's stopping you, when designing habit loops or trying to deploy them.

An example of a current paradigm is that of a Line Leader I once worked with who didn't address the need to change poor performance when they saw it. It was presented as a red performance indicator in a report or on a chart on the wall.

Their current view was they didn't want to ruffle feathers and they didn't want to reopen old debates. While believing they were doing the right thing, they were condoning poor performance which unintentionally or not, became the role modelled habit loop. In this situation, before being able to help them to deploy a new habit loop of challenging poor performance, it was necessary to unpick their current paradigm.

The fifth but very important final ingredient you need to build a new strong habit is focused practice with intensity and frequency.

You can't form a habit without frequent, consistent and focused practice; it is just not possible.

I x F = H

Intensity x Frequency = (New) Habit

The final ingredient you need to **build a new strong habit** is **focused practice** with **intensity and frequency.**

Coaching for World Class Organisations

You can read this book and form new habits with this recipe; however, if you want to be world-class, as many organisations aspire to be, then you need a coach. You'll struggle to find a world-class person who doesn't have a coach. Providing Coaching, in my view, is the role of the organisation, and we'll cover what's needed in Chapter 4.

A coach is someone who works with you to provide independent reflection in real-time and help you to hone the habitual pathways we've covered in this habit-building section. If you want to learn a new skill, for example, playing the guitar, you can watch YouTube clips and may be able to get yourself to a reasonable standard by practising with focus, intensity and frequency, but if you want to be a skilled or world-class guitarist, you can't do that on your own. You'll need coaching support to get to the next level.

The perfect scenario is to have these conditions in place, but at a bare minimum, I recommend having at least one person to support you. Have you ever tried giving up drinking or stopping smoking without support? If you have, you'll know how tough it is, which is why large organisations like Slimming World and Alcoholics Anonymous exist.

As you read the subsequent chapters, we will describe the habits you need for engagement. Your job is to figure out what is stopping you, the Cue, Routine and Reward, as well as the support cycle that builds intensity and frequency you will need to put in place to sustain these new habits in your circumstances and environment.

Trust

Trust is the other fundamental principle which must be present to build engagement because **Trust is at the heart of every good relationship.** Show me a relationship that isn't working, and I'll pinpoint a lack of trust. In my work as a consultant, and during my career as a leader, I often found myself working with businesses, teams and individuals, where the ability or desire to build engagement, was sabotaged by a conflict which was inevitably a result of a lack of trust. When I say **'conflict',** I don't mean war type conflict, but rather resentment which sits in the **'emotional backpack'** such as dissatisfaction, indifference or an unwillingness to cooperate. Irritation from unresolved issues continues to build in the emotional backpack which we'll talk more about in subsequent chapters. I have seen that Trust is too vital to not be at the centre of our engagement habits.

Every time we attempt to build these habits, we must do it with an understanding of Trust habits; they are linked, and one without the other not only doesn't work but also erodes engagement, stability, and sustainability. To build effective Engagement habits, you must role model Trust, irrespective of whether you're the CEO, head of an essential function, or a People Manager.

It sounds complicated, but like most things in life, it's easier than you think, and like all habits, mastery comes from frequent, focused practice.

I've broken Trust down into twelve clear and simple habits which we teach in our consulting, and I recommend you role model. You can see them in the following table.

Habit	Positive Role Model	Negative Role Model
1. Straight Talk	• Communicate with such clarity that you can't be misunderstood • Say it as it is - nicely • Leave lasting impressions	• Beating around the bush • Knowingly with-holding information • Leaving the wrong impressions
2. Respectful	• Treat others as you would want to be treated • Build 'LOVE' • A belief that everyone has a valuable contribution to make	• Being disrespectful • Don't put energy into caring • Accepting you don't care
3. Transparency	• Being as transparent as you can • Being open to feedback • Building a transparent structure	• Keeping secrets • Ignoring feedback • Hiding, covering up, purposefully not being transparent
4. Right Wrongs	• Genuinely apologise as a priority • Action your wrongs • Show humility	• Pretend your wrongs don't exist • Not admitting you're wrong until challenged • Putting yourself first
5. Being Loyal	• Credit where credit's due • Speaking about others as if they are present • Showing you're grateful	• Taking credit for others work • Backstabbing or criticising others • Not showing gratitude

6. Deliver Commitments	• Clarify expectations • Deliver on your commitments • Declare potential failure early enough to generate a positive outcome	• Avoid clarity and accountability • Fail against commitments • Hide failure
7. Continually Improve	• Hear feedback • Learn from mistakes • Push self to get better everyday	• Ignore or deflect feedback • Make the same mistakes • Stop striving for betterment
8. Confront Reality	• Confront tough issues appropriately • Share bad news when required • Discuss the elephant in the room	• Ignore the tough issues • Stay quiet when you know something needs saying • Allow others to ignore reality
9. Clarify Expectations	• Create clarity of expectation • Confirm what, where, when etc. when accepting accountability • Declare expectations	• Allow expectations to be undefined • Allow misaligned effort due to lack of clarity • Blame others when you don't meet expectations
10. Be Accountable	• Accept accountability • Admit/declare opportunities for it to be better • Be proactive	• Avoid accountability • Point fingers, blame others • Be a victim
11. Listen First	• Listen first, speak second • Listen without an agenda • Listen for what matters most to them	• Speak first, listen second • Drive your agenda without appreciating others • Listening with filters
12. Staying Committed	• Committing with clarity • Make, Keep, Repeat • Demonstrating delivery	• Breaking commitments without discussion • Manipulating commitment to suit you • Not accepting your commitments

These habits are founded on solid research by people such as Steven Covey and Steven M.R. Covey. In the table, we have identified each habit, as well as what a positive and a negative role model looks like, so you can recognise the results and behaviour that engender high levels of trust.

Finally, I want to share a version of The Trust Equation, which was first shared by Charles H. Green in the early 2000s. We have found this famous equation, not only to be accurate but also to be a useful way of measuring where you are on the scale, for a trusting relationship.

$$T = \frac{C \times R \times I}{S}$$

T: Trustworthiness; C: Credibility; R: Reliability; I: Intimacy; S: Self-Orientation

The Trust Equation

Credibility: This is whether people trust you as credible, and impacts whether they believe what you say.

Reliability: This is whether your actions are congruent with what you say. When you say something will get done, do you follow through?

Intimacy: This relates to how secure people feel in sharing their vulnerability with you. Do people trust you to keep their confidence, and not let them down?

Self-Orientation: This is about if you show up only for your agenda. Do people believe you are doing something to make yourself look good, or are you also present to support them?

When you look at relationships through the lens of this equation, it will give you a reliable guide to help you to decide where to focus your attention. Trust is variable and depends on the situation, and the value people place on the different areas of the equation.

A good example of this is when my mother, God rest her soul, had to have a major operation. The surgeon who was going to conduct the operation seemed to me like an obnoxious man, but, his credibility in his field was high, and he was considered one of the best surgeons in the country. This led me to believe he must also be reliable. I didn't warm to him, so the chances of me forming an intimate relationship with him were slim. But I thought that his Self-Orientation was at least partly in the right place because I could see that succeeding was critical to his reputation, which he obviously valued. While he may have been in it largely for his ego, I determined that he was also in it for my mother, because he couldn't maintain his excellent reputation without completing successful operations.

If you translate that into The Trust Equation terms, I had an overall level of Trust in him which although not high in every area of the equation, was particularly high in the areas of Reliability and Credibility which were the most critical factors in the situation because I didn't have to like him.

As we conclude this chapter, let's recap and summarise:

Now we have explained habits in theory; it is simple. True? Life and work is a set of habits, and all you have to do if you want to change is to reprogramme the habits. However, in practice, it isn't as simple as it sounds, but you now know what it takes to build a new habit and how to manage the existing ones. In future chapters, as well as describing the habits you require for high engagement, we will provide a few examples, so look out for these at the end of each subsequent chapter.

Life and work is a set of habits, and all you have to do if you want to change is to reprogramme the habits.

As for the principle of Trust, irrespective of our role, we all know deep down in our gut that it is essentially easier, more enjoyable and more rewarding when work is undertaken in an environment of high trust. If you are the CEO or the most senior leader within the business; like it or not, it is your job to set the tone of the trust environment you wish to have in your business. It is my experience that you will be placed upon a trust pedestal whether you ask for it or not.

People will be looking at you through the lens of the Trust Equation (although they may not know it) and will either knock you off it or keep you on it, based purely on the four factors of The Trust Equation. You have to be able to demonstrate all four if you want people to follow you.

For the central function and The People Manager, your position in role modelling trust cannot be underestimated; you are the point at which trust becomes tangible and real for people on a daily basis. You are the mirror that is reflecting the trust environment of the organisation, and this means building trust habits isn't optional but imperative.

With this in mind, as you move forward with this book, I would like you to consider two things:

The first is **how you turn these insights into a habit** because only if they become **habitual will they be repeatable and sustainable.**

The second is about **how to do it in a trusting way**; a way that **provides a strong foundation for The Engagement Habit.**

Life and work is a **set of habits,** and all you have to do if you want to change is to **reprogramme the habits.**

The CEO's Paradigm

Section 1: You Are the Culture Catalyst

CEOs, business owners, site directors: it's for anyone who leads the culture. For ease of reference, I'll refer to them as the CEO.

Fair or not, your role has a disproportionate impact. You're the lightning rod for everything good, or more typically, everything bad that happens in the organisation. Have you ever been blamed for car parking problems at work? It may seem unfair, but that's the way it goes; you're the lightning rod.

I remember when Christer Hollaman launched Glassdoor.com in Europe, and he introduced us to a rating called **"Approve of the CEO"**. My CEO was bemused by the rating and wondered how such a judgement could be made. He questioned whether the outcome could be a measure of the CEO or a measure of the company and whether the distinction was important. As he pointed out, 'most of those who make the judgement have never even met me!'

I'm writing this at the time of the COVID-19 lockdown. Everyone has an opinion of the UK Prime Minister, Boris Johnson, and whether he wanted it or not, he's been thrust into the role of culture Catalyst. He's the catalyst for our society. He's the 21st century Churchill, fighting an invisible enemy. Social media is full of people making judgements about his leadership when, in reality, he's simply the focal point for a huge team of ministers, civil servants and government experts. His mood, his mannerisms, his words and his tone, impact the morale and the confidence of the nation at this time of national emergency. He's there to provide direction. Citizens of the UK need to have faith he will protect us. And similarly, whether you like it or not, as the leader of the business, you set the tone; you create the culture of humanity, caring and togetherness or, in some cases, ruthlessness, individualism and politics. It's all down to you.

Section 2: The Culture Leader

Do you already recognise your role as the leader of culture? My professional career started in the late 1980s when the role of the CEO was to manage the numbers. I distinctly remember my first brush with a CEO when I received a phone call late one evening asking me to explain a number he had spotted in a lengthy report. My definition of a CEO changed in an instant to someone who had the detail-consciousness to be on top of every single number. Calling a junior manager at home in the evening was acceptable by the standards of the time. As the decades progressed, the role of the CEO morphed into a focus on the market: the customers, the brand and the company's reputation.

CEOs were seemingly oblivious to what was happening outside the head office. The launch of Engage for Success in 2011 allowed me to start a different conversation with a selection of CEOs and business leaders. In one of the early studies, our task force looked at engagement through the CEO's eyes. We interviewed sixteen UK chairman and CEOs, to get a snapshot of how well the business leaders understood employee engagement.

While some discussed engagement in terms of people and emotion, many described it as a transactional process; a formal dialogue or an activity centred around pulse and staff surveys and town hall meetings. Others talked about engagement in terms of a formal consultation process, job design and career ladders, while the more progressive, viewed engagement as a long-term process. There were varied and conflicting viewpoints which made our mission all the more challenging.

It was around this time that I started hearing the phrase "culture-shaping". The Engage for Success team identified issues which acted as barriers to CEOs shaping culture: Short-term focus, executive incentives, historical criteria for career development, organisational hierarchies, and a range of what management theory would call structural factors.

For me, it's simpler than that. In my experience, two things stop CEOs embracing their role as the culture shaper. The first is the **fear of engaging** because this means you **have to let people in and show your vulnerability.** I remember a Managing Director I worked for, telling me he didn't need to be human because he had a Human Resources Director to do it for him!

The second is the **belief that they cannot influence the whole organisation.** I sympathise, but the root of this fear is that they haven't understood the potential of **'The Shadow of the Leader',** which is one of the principles of the work we do in transforming employee engagement within organisations.

Section 3: The Shadow of the Leader

It's been my experience that over time, the management and organisational culture of any group, changes to reflect the style of the leader. I've seen this across the board in small informal groups of twenty, right up to multinational organisations of 150,000 people. The time it takes for the change to occur depends on a variety of factors such as business size, geographical distribution and corporate history.

Whether it's because of the natural human desire to fit in and model the behaviour of the most influential person, or whether it's down to the power of story-telling which creates and proliferates legend and rumour, eminent social science studies have been written about this phenomenon. I would guess that you have many examples in your professional or personal life that bear this point out. Whether your sports team has changed because of the style of the coach, or the performance of your kids' school has improved because of a charismatic new head teacher, this is one of those things that we see as common sense, but in business we underplay the significance and look instead for system and structural initiatives.

The surprise phone call from the CEO I referred to earlier, was the most impactful incident in my entire decade with that company. Twenty years on and I still clearly remember the chilling experience when the CEO sternly asked me to explain what to me was a seemingly obscure statistic on page twenty-seven of the report. The clear message was that you had to be in control of the detail, and you must also be available eighteen hours a day whether in the office or at home.

The CEO operated that way, and so his senior managers copied him, and they expected me to do the same. What to the CEO was just a routine phone call, to me was a test from the most powerful person in the business, on whether I fit in and had what it took for the long-term. Such is the shadow of the leader and how they set the pace.

In comparison, later in my career, I worked for Airbus, a company fuelled by the zeal of European cooperation and the dream of growth and innovation. They were designing and building the impossible; the goal was to build the giant A380 aircraft, which appeared to defy the laws of physics. After years of being led by French Le Grande L'ecole graduates, steeped in French orthodoxy and bureaucracy, Airbus was now piloted by a young German ex-paratrooper, a man with a reputation similar to that of James Bond. The legend was he went for a parachute jump every lunchtime. His Personal Assistant would nervously break the news he may be late due to weather conditions. A sense of daring, boldness and risk-taking, underpinned by camaraderie, permeated the organisation. The culture of the company became human and charismatic. Wearing ties instantly became old fashioned. When the CEO communicated, staff would hang on his every word. The core of his communication style was a desire to succeed together, and his positivity and empathy were infectious.

Suitable systems, policies and values must underpin the shadow of the leader. Still, the behaviour of the leader has a profound impact on how senior leaders act, which in turn, trickles down throughout the organisation. It is about you: the CEO.

Throughout this book, we focus on habits, particularly the habit loop of the cue-routine reward. Another way of describing the shadow of the leader is to think of the CEO as **the most influential and frequent provider of the cue,** whether intentional or unintentional. Every action, behaviour and decision produces a cue which triggers people's routines.

Every action, behaviour and decision produces a cue which triggers people's routines.

To begin changing the current culture, CEOs must first accept responsibility for how it is being created and become aware of the cues they are transmitting to their organisation.

Section 4: You Can't Delegate Culture.

I already mentioned the now-outdated model of the CEO who believed their job was to manage the numbers, and how it was followed by the next evolution, where the focus switched to the brand and customer. In 2010, I noticed that CEOs started to recognise the importance of culture and to issue instructions to specialists in their organisations to fix their culture problem.

This created a dynamic where the CEO was satisfied that culture was being taken care of, whilst the specialist beavered away creating endless plans. As a Human Resources Director, I too succumbed to the seduction of participating in board meetings where I would dutifully present our people progress plans at the end of the session.

Human beings spot inauthenticity a mile off, so when observing 'how things get done around here', they are influenced by the CEO's behaviour and habits far more than what's written in the company literature.

In this example, the CEO fell into the trap of trying to delegate culture, which can't be done. **You can't buy culture either. As long as the facilities are satisfactory, no number of fancy accessories and office pool tables will disguise the say-do gap.**

Customers regularly present new challenges, and for this reason,

your people must think on their feet.

The role modelling of the CEO, trumps everything else, every time.

Section 5: What Should You Do?

There is a wealth of resources on what I call the 'So What' topic, from leadership development institutions to Harvard Business Review. In the spirit of this being a practical guide, I'm not going to attempt to give you a better official summary than INSEAD Business School or Harvard Business Review. I'm also not going to waste your time with another 'new' leadership framework for you to copy. Instead, I'll share the key 'CEO Habits', I've seen in my career which have had the most significant impact on building a culture of engagement. My suggestions are designed to spark your thinking so you think about and design your own habits which will naturally be tailor-made for your situation.

CEO Habits

Habit 1: Provide a compass, not a map.

Remember; People Protect What They Build. Leadership is characterised by initiative and action. It traditionally presents an example for others to follow, a route to a particular place. As leaders, our instinct is to take our teams by the hand and help them safely across the battlefield. Our logic is to show them how to do what we managed to do, and it's natural to want to save them from common landmines. We have the belief that if we did it, they can too. Isn't it the

responsibility of the leader to explain to others the best method to achieve the goal?

The problem with this approach is **there is no such thing as one map to reach any goal.** There are numerous possibilities to navigate the route and to arrive at the desired destination. As the leader, we may never have even considered alternate routes. When our aim is to have the team duplicate our route, we may consult a route planner and provide a list of directions. This is great when everything happens exactly as anticipated.

The major flaw in this method is in the nature of life's unpredictability. You have probably noticed that even with detailed planning, events rarely unfold as we anticipate!

What if one day there's a traffic jam or a road closure? I once drove from the North of the UK to Limoges in Southern France, relying on a printout of route directions from AA Route Planner. Once I arrived on the other side of the Channel Tunnel, I took one wrong turn and the plan became instantly obsolete. If your people are prepared for one route only, how will they cope when they encounter a diversion and are unable to follow the meticulous plan?

They won't be mentally prepared to face the unknown. **Customers regularly present new challenges,** and for this reason, **your people must think on their feet.** Allow them to make mistakes and learn for themselves; otherwise, one significant change in direction and a step-by-step prescription is immediately rendered useless. If, however, you provide your people with a compass and give them the ownership to figure out the journey, they can learn to read the signs along the way and will be able to reach true north, whatever they encounter along the way.

In practical terms, this means that **as the leader, your job is not to explain the steps to achieve the task, but to be clear about the generally non-negotiable destination.** Be ready to give guidance so your people won't take unnecessary and potentially dangerous risks that you can help them to avoid, but apart from issues of safety, stand back and manage from a distance. This takes self-discipline if you're used to a different leadership style, but it is a new habit that will pay-off in terms of productivity, peace of mind and employee engagement. Like any new habit, the first few times you try something new, it may be unsettling but the reward will be worth the initial discomfort.

People crave autonomy, and they develop by solving problems on their own. Mistakes will be made, but they only serve to strengthen the learning process and are a worthy investment of time and patience.

> Mistakes will be made, but they strengthen the learning process and are a worthy investment of time and patience.

Over time people will grow from the experience of figuring it out, and because it is their method (not yours) they will feel greater ownership for its sustainment and improvement.

As covered in Chapter I, the first Principle is People Protect What They Build, and our consulting work revolves around this understanding. Allow people to work out the route; they'll be more committed to reaching the destination, and they'll be proud of their progress. As the leader, you don't need to know the detail of their route, their relationships, their role and their unique challenges.

Habit 2: Nurture your circle of safety.

Humans are social animals. Deep in our evolutionary makeup, we are hardwired to rely on each other to protect ourselves against danger. We do not have sharp teeth or plated skin, what we do have are innate superpowers to collaborate, innovate, and problem-solve. This gives us the ability not only to be shaped by the environment but to shape our environment to stay safe.

We've evolved so that when we trust those in our circles of safety, we will share information and ideas to strengthen our group against outside dangers. Social scientists and anthropologists state that the most effective circles of safety rely on leaders whose role it is to protect them and to create an environment of stability and harmony where collaboration flourishes. It makes no sense to fight one another inside our own circles. It didn't work in The Lion King, and it won't work in your organisation. In the years following the financial crisis of 2008, and inevitably in the years following the COVID-19 pandemic, for many companies, managing, restructuring and downsizing will become a core management discipline. In these situations, employee engagement becomes even more vital. Employees look to leaders for their circle of safety. Simon Sinek explains the concept of the circle brilliantly. He talks about the daily threats businesses face and the launch of new disruptive technology that can take your industry by storm overnight, which can result in emerging competing brands dominating your market.

Innovation is a product of taking risks and frequently failing. If failing is discouraged within your organisation, or punishable by losing your job, employees won't venture to try new things because of the fear of the consequences.

This is where good leaders shine.

It's essential your teams have the utmost confidence in their job stability and also feel they have the freedom to work autonomously. If they don't have confidence in the company, there'll be paralysed by fear, afraid to innovate and problem solve. As CEO, one of your key roles is to provide that stability, a belief that the company will do the right thing and protect your team.

Early in my career, I was involved in closing a large aerospace factory. The Managing Director made it his mission to redeploy, or at least to offer a solution for each of the 790 employees. He would chair a daily review of a large spreadsheet which tracked whether each person would leave through voluntary redundancy, or be redeployed to a different site within the group. Each day the meeting became shorter as the spreadsheet shrunk, however, even in the final days when only a couple of people remained, he carried on meticulously honouring his commitment to creating a plan for every single person. This became legendary across the whole company.

During future factory closures or periods of job losses, employees would say there was no need to worry because they were confident the company would look after them. The leader had created a circle of safety in a difficult time when people were at their most insecure and this is a brilliant example of leadership at its finest.

As the CEO, you have the authority to habitualise this level of caring, but because of the 'shadow of the leader' you also have tremendous power to role model this particular habit.

How often do you praise people for a valiant attempt or for something that they did not believe they could have done the day before? By making this a daily habit, you will quickly spread this throughout your leadership and create a 'circle of safety' which allows people to try new things, take risks and develop their skills.

Habit 3: Know your people and let them know you.

How well do you know your team? I met the Managing Director of a large retail chain who memorised the first names of every employee in the company stores as well as one thing about their personal life. The reason he did so was that he wanted an effective way of starting a conversation so his staff would know he cared. He would also share basic information about himself, such as the name of his wife. I was amazed at how informed he was about the current challenges in the stores. Due to the genuine connection he had formed with each of the employees, he was able to focus on problem-solving while skilfully evaluating when they had more to offer or when they needed additional support.

On another occasion, I was charged with leading a team who were going through a particularly tough period of change, which potentially put all of our jobs in jeopardy. I briefed the team regularly and noticed one member seemed to be undermining the change process with her repeated probing questions.

I decided to take a listen first approach, to try and understand her concerns. I discovered her husband had recently been made redundant; she was now the sole breadwinner for her young family. Suddenly her forensic questioning made perfect sense – she was not just asking for herself, she was trying to anticipate and be in a position to answer questions her family would ask her each evening. By patiently communicating with her to identify her concerns, she grew to trust me, and our team briefings began to run smoothly. The other team members recognised my genuine empathy, and my efforts resulted in a stronger relationship with her and the team.

Throughout the past ten years, many senior leaders have begun blogging. By writing a regular blog, with a section devoted to something personal such as the hobby of the leader, they can create a sense of community in the organisation, in a similar way to how the retail chain manager found conversation starters with all of his staff.

One CEO blogged about his football team who endured a terrible thrashing at the weekend. By giving his team a glimpse of his personal life, before meetings, they would ask him about the game. As a result, meetings started with people smiling, rather than dreading what was to come. I remember one blog where an MD made a point of outlining a particular challenge. He was happy to say that he was stumped, and just didn't know the answer. Within a few days, I heard members of his team say something similar about issues they were facing, which put them in the position where they could ask for opinions and support.

Whilst this may sound like a simple thing, surely many of the day to day problems we face are new to us all, the paradigm in that organisation, and most I have witnessed, is one where the big bosses act as though they have all of the answers, and as a result, asking for help is seen as a weakness.

Another example is that of a Managing Director who blogged about a mental health issue he was dealing with in his family. Mental Health had been a 'corporate initiative' for a number of years, with features in the company magazine and posters sharing the internal helpline at every briefing station. That single emotional and personal blog dissolved the taboo of mental health in the company. It's a powerful example of how sharing your humanity at work makes a big difference.

On the flip side, I also remember one Managing Director describing how he spent the weekend working on his Maserati. As you may imagine, this didn't resonate as well as he'd hoped!

This is a simple, but profound habit to practice. **It is amazing how sharing your humanity and being vulnerable, allows others to connect with you on a deeper level.** This powerful cue will change the conversation; both your personal exchanges as well as the conversation in the organisation. The reward is that over time a more open culture will emerge.

NEVER

underestimate the **value of making time for your people.**

Habit 4: Allow time to engage.

Every business leader has a list of mandatory tasks; those necessary activities to get their job done. But if a leader's role is client strategy, it's more challenging to achieve the desired outcome without new data on what the company's doing. While leaders believe their job is to get stuff done, they prioritise their to-do list and underestimate the importance of investing time and energy into the areas of the business that arguably need it the most.

As a result, the time allocated for engaging with staff gets pushed onto the back burner in favour of something urgent. It then typically turns into a rushed conversation in the hallway.

Never underestimate the value of making time for your people. We all have an innate desire to be heard, so it's a great idea to block-out your engagement time before your other tasks. Apart from boosting your employee engagement it also, with no additional effort, makes you more productive because you'll know exactly what's happening in your organisation, rather than trying to push blindly through your to-do list.

I'm currently working with a director of a large national defence programme. He has planned his diary so that he spends mornings in the business and afternoons working on the business. In practical terms, what this means is he spends the morning walking around his facility, talking to people. He does this with two goals in mind: the first is to get to know his staff (habit 3) to the point where he's confident they trust him to be honest about what's actually going on. And the second is to describe his vision to the people and translate it into words that are relevant to them, thus giving them the opportunity to build (habits I and 5). Although it may seem as though it takes more time; he's found it to be incredibly productive. He is far better informed when he reviews reports and talks to people about specific issues and is therefore equipped to make the right decisions.

Initially, this was a very difficult habit to experiment with. Like all leaders, he was 'too busy' to prioritise talking to his team. Over time, he has found that it is a far more effective use of time. What previously was an hour reading a report or reviewing a PowerPoint presentation is now accomplished in a fraction of the time by identifying the issue at its source. He has also found that by asking a few questions, he can empower the person to resolve it. This has made the adoption of the habit pay for itself many times over, and the rewards are significant for his team, in terms of engagement.

You'll be familiar with the importance of putting customers first, but **put your employees first**, and as a result, **great customer service will naturally follow.**

One of the most excellent examples of using information and data to define the direction of a company, such as price, investment and stocking decisions, is the Tesco Club Card. Many of us have or have had one of these membership cards where Tesco intelligently mines personal data about us, our shopping habits, shopping timings etc. You, as the CEO, are positioned like the Tesco Club Card programme, but you won't gather this data by hiding away in your office.

This information is a goldmine for your organisation and the only way to mine its full potential is to engage with your people personally.

Habit 5: Never miss an opportunity to connect people with your vision.

In our consultancy, Mark and I often come across leaders who talk at great length about how difficult it is to connect their employees with the direction, strategy and vision the business is working towards. When we ask how often they talk about their vision with the team, they tell us not much. When we delve deeper, we discover that they point to some kind of graphic at the start of meetings, or a statement of intent etched into the glass in their reception area. The problem is that visions don't come alive by looking at a poster on the wall. You have to take every opportunity to connect your people with the big picture of your vision. Pick up any book on change management, and it will talk about the importance of connecting employees with the vision. I've found this to be true with every client. The vision has to be explained and translated so that your people grasp the vision for themselves.

Dan Pink talks about purpose, autonomy, and mastery when he describes how people are motivated. Purpose is about connecting people with a vision. In our client work in a defence programme; it's evident whether people are connected with the company vision, when you walk around and ask them what they're up to. Those who have internalised the vision, describe what they're doing in the context of the overall objectives of their team and in relation to the vision. Those who haven't connected with the vision, describe the transactional activity in which they're involved. To some, many of whom are ex service personnel the purpose of what they are doing is to support those who are still serving; returning them to a safe and functional boat. To others it is to deliver a great job which strengthens the future of the site where their sons and daughters are doing apprenticeships.

To translate the vision effectively, the boss has to understand how that individual will find purpose, something that will only come from human conversation.

A great example of someone who found real purpose in their job was the Apollo 13 worker. When asked how he was getting on as he swept the floor, he said he was putting a man on the moon. Now that's connection with a vision! Every employee, no matter their role, can be engaged in the vision by showing them how their work impacts the big picture.

Remember, as the CEO; you are the culture catalyst.

Habit 6: Focus on your company's voice.

Companies invest a lot of time thinking about their external brand voice; the way their company comes across to potential clients. This is important because the type of brand voice you use has a significant impact on the number of sales you make.

However, companies spend little or no time talking about their internal brand voice. Consider what culture you want in your company, and what tone of voice complements it.

Circling back to the CEO of Airbus: the young German ex-paratrooper, his internal company communication permeated the organisation and created an environment where people felt as though they were taking part in a mission that transcended the day to day objectives. When considering your company's internal voice, remember that authenticity is vital. Don't be afraid to be honest and to show vulnerability. Be direct, talk straight. You'd be surprised how well people accept challenging news when you're honest and don't treat them like fools.

You are in charge of setting the tone of voice for the company; how you speak, and how you communicate through blogs and emails will quickly be replicated

by your senior management and organisation. What tone of voice do you want to replicate?

If we think back to the Trust we spoke about in chapter two, you will recall the high trust habits and what role modelling these meant in terms of engagement. A positive role model for **'Straight Talk'**, for example, is clarity of communication; how you say it and the impression you leave. Now what would that say about your company's voice?

Habit 7: Be a servant leader.

There is a considerable amount of research around the concept of servant leadership or what is sometimes described as the inverted triangle. You've probably read some of it and perhaps attended a course. Firstly, when you're talking to your people, keep in mind that your role as the CEO isn't to only transmit. To impact your employee engagement, it's critical that you also listen and learn.

As the Greek philosopher, Epictetus said, **"We have two ears and one mouth so that we can listen twice as much as we speak."**.

> "We have two ears and one mouth so that we can listen twice as much as we speak."
>
> Epictetus

Remember that every conversation you have with a member of your team is a coaching opportunity. For many leaders, this is a difficult habit to adopt, having spent many years in 'transmit mode'.

As we already covered, People Protect What They Build, so encourage them to come up with ideas and develop insights and solutions. You are in charge of all of the organisation's resources, and as such you are also the integration point, by which I mean all of the functions of the business ultimately report to you. When I talk to people, whether on a manufacturing floor, in a call centre or a retail outlet, I frequently hear that people can't proceed because they are waiting for an activity to be performed by another department or function. As the chief integration and escalation point in the business, you can eliminate these bottlenecks by letting your people know you expect them to collaborate across departmental and functional boundaries.

The trick here is not to go and fix it yourself, but to think about how you engender an environment of cross functional working where those on the front line are truly supported by everyone else in the organisation. If this is your expectation, how do you ensure that everyone realises it? Make it a habit to find out how your front-line teams can be supported, and encourage those who should support their own people, to do so. After a number of requests for them to provide support, often they will begin to do it automatically because it becomes a habit. You will quickly create a situation where it is an expectation that the organisation is there to support those closest to the customer, or those who are on the front line.

Servant Leadership is a habit, and it is habitualised not through words, but through deeds.

Habit 8: Reinforce accountability.

Much of what we've talked about so far may give you the impression that employee engagement is simply about being nice to people. While I would encourage you to be nice, your role is to achieve great performance outcomes for your business. To be an effective CEO, **you must be clear in your expectations and be highly proficient in articulating them clearly.** When you are talking to members of your team and getting in the habit of maximising coaching opportunities, people will begin to share their ideas freely, and what they plan to do. This is where you can convey the expectation that this is a commitment they've made to you.

Don't hesitate to return at an appropriate time to ask them how they got on and to either commend them on their follow-through, or challenge them if they've not done what they said they would.

Part of your role in creating the culture in the organisation is to develop a culture of expectation where when people make commitments; you expect them to be honoured.

To achieve higher performance, ensure that for every necessary action, it's clear who is accountable for ensuring it is delivered, and what the 'promise date' is for completion. Create that expectation and hold people to account.

Mark and I, spend a great deal of time in organisations, writing and committing to regular objectives. In my experience, the best organisations are those where regular daily, or hourly commitments are delivered. Programme performance is achieved through timely delivery of thousands of daily commitments, customer excellence is delivered through hundreds of customer commitments.

Delivery against commitments becomes a desirable habit, and as the CEO, you are in the position to make it an expectation.

When thinking about building a new engagement habit it is useful to write down your response to the five elements we spoke about in Chapter 2. Here is an example that may help your thinking.

Example for Habit 4: Allow Time to Engage

1: The Current Paradigm	2: Cue	3: Routine	4: Reward	5: Focused Practice
What's going to stop me building the new habit?	What will trigger the new habit loop I want?	What is the pathway I wish to follow?	What will make me do it again?	When and how?
I am too busy, I don't have time I try but other things always come into play and stop me Other priorities outside my control absorb my time	Reserved time that is blocked out in the diary weekly A diary review on a Sunday evening for 15mins that recentres the importance of the time to engage A message to myself on my desk A colleague reminds me each day	I declare each week that I will be unavailable at this specific time Each day I remind myself of the time I have set aside to engage When something tries to cut across that time I: • Say no and offer an alternative time • Say yes and reprioritise so something else drops out of the diary for this week	I get to know the people I am leading The people I am leading get to know me and the vision we have for the business I understand first hand the great things about our business and the not-so-great things I have greater insight into where the leadership efforts of the business should be focused I will feel better about knowing in greater detail the opportunities and risks	Weekly I will do it with my local leader in the area I visit I shall feedback to the local team and my direct report what I felt, saw and heard

You MUST be **clear in your expectations** and be highly proficient in articulating them clearly.

The Organisation's Response

Most of my career has been spent in big engineering businesses where I've been involved in Process Reengineering, Total Quality Management, Lean and Kaizen. I've used these as a vehicle to drive higher engagement and ownership of work at the appropriate levels. I've personally seen the power of participation in continuous improvement to dramatically increase productivity in a range of industries from rail, aircraft jet manufacture to shipyards.

From the early days, my view of a central role, such as HR, was to enable the culture that unleashed people's ideas and potential. I didn't label the role as engagement because I always thought that engagement was the means rather than the end product.

As I shared in the previous chapters, I participated in the Engage for Success Taskforce; a UK government-led initiative, which aimed to operationalise the work of David MacLeod and Nita Clarke.

The Prime Minister, David Cameron, launched the taskforce saying, 'I'm delighted the employee engagement taskforce has come together to develop practical ways to help employers learn from the best, to break down barriers to engagement and to raise the profile of the whole agenda.'

I led the task force work on maintaining morale through difficult challenges such as downsizing, which became critical as the economy wrestled with the impact of the crash, following the sub-prime catastrophe.

Around the same time, I was asked to move into a group role as employee relations and engagement director. The first element of this role: employee relations, was well established. BAE Systems was heavily unionised with mature consultation mechanisms involving unions and other social partners. The second element: engagement, was new; the organisation had not previously had an 'engagement lead'.

I was initially sceptical, but my boss was insistent and persuaded me it was of critical importance. Our CEO was a sponsor of Engage for Success which meant all of the divisional MDs were clear that engagement was now a key objective. I'm confident that when I was appointed some of the MDs and HR leaders let out a palpable sigh of relief! They were relieved to return to their day jobs, safe in the knowledge that they had passed the engagement ball on to someone else, and they wouldn't need to worry about it any longer. Soon I was in high demand with people calling on me to ask for input on a whole range of things such as board papers, annual reports and corporate social responsibility statements. Members of the graduate scheme nervously called me, asking for the latest pearls of wisdom to include in their dissertation. External requests would be fielded from auditors and insurers as engagement became the buzz word for the corporate governance community.

Big organisations operate within a paradigm where central functions exist to lead agendas. If the word 'engagement' is in your job title, you may already have noticed that you're somehow responsible for fixing anything and everything related to it!

When I entered the world of consulting, I had the opportunity to work with a range of 'central function' people in many different companies; large and small. I assumed that in smaller companies, the business leaders would be closer to their people, so 'people management' would be what they naturally did, and functions like HR wouldn't be expected to drive 'people'. I have found a great deal of variability, with many MDs and CEOs being excellent leaders; however, there are still a fair few small and medium-size companies where the HR lead is still very much expected to 'make people engaged'!

In my time as a HR Director, an Engagement Director, and latterly as a consultant, I think **I have come across many of the 'myths' that surround engagement.** In many organisations, these myths form a decent chunk of the job description of the HR or Engagement specialist. For those reading this in those roles, I wonder how many of these you may recognise!

The 6 Myths of Engagement

Myth 1: We must have an engagement plan.

This myth might sound like heresy. The paradigm in the companies I worked for, demanded that for anything important there must be a company-wide strategy of what you're trying to achieve and why, and a company-wide plan, which defines what you intend to do.

While it's a good thing to have clarity on what the organisation aims to achieve and why, all of my experience shows that **positive change around engagement, comes from the bottom-up activity, and is built and owned at a local level.** Having a company-wide engagement plan smacks of building the roof before the foundation.

For many people caught up in the rush for an engagement plan to satisfy their company's initiative culture, it can feel counter intuitive, and they already realise that one size does not fit all.

I can hear a former boss, as if perched on my shoulder as I write, saying, 'But what about the employee value proposition (EVP)?'

If you're one of the few companies to have a single EVP, some structural things such as reward, talent and process, may share a clear commonality. However, engagement is a participation sport, and it's forged between people, not created on paper.

Myth 2: You can make someone engaged.

The root of most of the engagement myths which drive central teams in their quest for central engagement plans is the mistaken belief that the company can engage. When I coach line managers, particularly those new to people management, I ask them who they think motivated them. After further discussion and after considering parents, old bosses and those who initially trained them, they typically see that the only person who can motivate them is themselves.

Nobody drives anyone else; we have been led to believe through a misunderstanding of human behaviour, that external motivation is the holy grail. The reality is that **we can create favourable conditions for people to be motivated, but the motivation must ultimately come from within: it's an inside-out job.** If I asked you to list three situations where you were engaged, I suspect the circumstances would comprise a variety of factors such as the company, the market, the CEO and the company's mission statement. The situations you would probably list are activities, the people around you, and the feeling of personal ownership.

While some examples may include a direct boss, if you were to transfer the same tasks and people to another company, many would be equally engaged. As I have grown older, I have learnt what I need to be highly engaged in a task. It does not matter whether this is a company project, a household chore or a hobby. The things that get me going are clear to me and very different from those that engage the next person. It is the employee who is the differentiating factor.

Organisations: usually their direct line managers, set up the environment for engagement to occur, but by far, the most significant factor is whether the individual chooses to engage. Engagement is a choice. If we accept this premise, it's obvious why many of the assumptions around engagement are fundamentally flawed.

> **Engagement is unlikely to be delivered by a company-wide action plan, the response to a survey by a well-meaning executive team, an enthusiastic HR function or a set of one-size fits-all reward mechanisms.**

Myth 3: Engagement is a top-down process.

Another belief that dogs the engagement topic is that for change to happen, it can only be driven from the top. While senior executive engagement buy in is desirable, my experience is that positive change comes when senior managers don't attempt to drive engagement but instead, allow and encourage it.

As in the previous myth, if you accept that engagement isn't something that one person does to another, the best a company can hope for is to create the ideal environment to foster it. You would be wise not to invest, design and produce a product for a market you don't understand, and engagement is the same. Allow it to naturally flourish in the relationships between individuals who understand each other. As you will soon see, the required conditions are most successfully created through habits, not structures.

Myth 4: What gets measured gets managed

Ever attended a meeting where you look at the results of the employee survey and conclude that not a lot has changed? I've experienced the soul destroying process of spending millions of company pounds on surveys designed to summarise the average viewpoint of tens of thousands of employees. Grey suited executives (of which I have been one) then apply their own interpretation to the data and create their company-wide action plan.

I once remember one of my team who set up a mid-survey pulse process. He encouraged team managers to spend one hour per month in conversation with his or her team, asking a couple of questions, typically found in the main survey and then working out what, as a group, they could do to improve their lot. After initial scepticism, the teams engaged, and a mini engine of improvement was created in that business area. That was a worthwhile exercise.

I'm diabetic. Every year I go and see a nurse who explains the stats from my blood tests. I understand what each of the statistics means because I've had these tests for many years. However, nothing in my understanding changes my long-term prognosis.

The fact that it does not change it doesn't mean it's a waste of time. It's what I do about the results that make the difference. My test results are what's important because when I have those, I can agree on a course of action with my doctor. Interestingly, the statistics of all the diabetics surveyed in the country are also largely irrelevant to my health.

Likewise, with company surveys; if you must do a survey, I suggest you do what my team member did. Create an exercise that specifically seeks to understand the individuals in your team and then agree on a plan of action. To increase employee engagement, set it up so that ownership for the desired change belongs to the individual.

Just as the results for the diabetics in the UK have little impact on my situation, neither do the results of an employee survey which averages and then publishes company statistics from 100,000 employees.

Myth 5: You can perk your way to engagement.

A popular belief is that you can recruit the best people by offering juicy perks such as; pool tables, a dry-cleaning service and complimentary access to the vending machine. Perks do not drive lasting engagement. Psychologists have proven that once people get a positive outcome, their expectations quickly adapt to the new reality. It's called Adaptation Theory.

Perks do not encourage the underlying drivers of engagement. They may give a temporary boost to the employee, and you might feel like a better employer, but in the long-term, they do not improve company engagement.

Myth 6: Engagement is the job of HR

Now you understand the other myths; it's clear why Engagement is not the job of HR. HR can play a vital role in the conversation, share learning and good practice across the company, and can drive a few structural things to reinforce and sustain good engagement which is already happening. **HR can also coach and facilitate the coaching of engagement habits in the line.** However, engagement should not be outsourced to HR.

What Should Central Functions Do?

The first and most obvious job for central functions is to debunk these myths. As someone whose professional career developed through the period where central functions were routinely described as an 'overhead', I recognise that it is tough to argue that things that you are asked to provide are not required. At times, avoiding the repeated requests for a company-wide engagement plan felt like guerrilla warfare, instead deciding to support leaders around me to adopt the kind of habits described in other chapters of this book. I also recognise that coaching leaders to adopt habits is 'hard yards' in comparison to designing a company wide initiative. As described in a previous chapter, building new habits requires intensity and frequency.

Perhaps if I can use a comparison to illustrate the point: In the early days of discussing engagement, a typical company response was to communicate, in particular, to explain the company objectives so that our people could work out how to create 'shareholder value'. If you subscribe to the opinion that we are more engaged if the company's mission is meaningful to us, which I do, surely this must be an entirely logical thing for a company to do.
I fully subscribe to the importance of the company doing, what Nita and David call, 'creating a strategic narrative', but does it provide meaning for employees?

The only people who can find meaning are the employees themselves. I mentioned in a previous chapter, the programme director I worked with who sees one of his goals as ensuring his team understand the objectives. For some, the objective; of getting a submarine ready for service is about providing their ex-colleagues; many of whom are ex-submariners, the ability to return home from their tour of duty.

For others, the objective is to secure the reputation of the programme with a view to ongoing employment for their family members or local apprentices. Others simply don't want to let down their mates who work on the next team in the production process.

My point is that 'meaningful work' is different for each person. What the programme director does beautifully is to explain the programme objectives and give team members the freedom to find their own meaning. When I observe him in action, I see that 90%

of the conversation involves him listening. The other 10% is him asking carefully considered questions. This engagement is personal, tailored and happens through a human connection.

It's a great illustration of how engagement happens and provides a clear contrast to the model of company communications that we are all so used to. It is just too easy to create material (communications material, policy and process, action plans, etc.) and then email them out, assuming that they will be willingly accepted and adopted by others. This approach is based on a number of the myths outlined above – it is based on the paradigm that you can make people engaged, that it is the job of the company to engage people top down, that it is the job of the central function to take the lead on that and that the most effective way of doing this is a 'one size fits all' centrally designed and planned approach.

Where in the last chapter, a key message to the CEO was not to delegate culture, a key message to the central functions has to be not to accept the delegation.

> A key message to the CEO is to not delegate culture, a key message to the central functions is to not accept the delegation.

Push back, bust the myths and do not accept the myths I have described in this section, but instead support the CEO to deploy the habits that will make his or her shadow the most positive it can be and support people managers to deploy the kind of game-changing habits that we will explore in the next chapters.

Your role is to be the thought leader for engagement, working out what habits to encourage and to discourage, and most importantly, to be the coach who supports people managers along that journey.

No sports person ever became world-class by diligently reading the manual on sporting technique – they become great by working with a great coach, helping them to build great habits and practice them with support, guidance and challenge.

This is your role, so get out and coach!

Example of a Habit in support of debunking the myths

Myth 1: we must have an Engagement plan

1: The Current Paradigm	2: Cue	3: Routine	4: Reward	5: Focused Practice
What's going to stop me building the new habit?	What will trigger the new habit loop I want?	What is the pathway I wish to follow?	What will make me do it again?	When and how?
The organisation and leadership desire one plan I don't have the capacity to do something different My boss won't let me	The request for one plan The current success we are having around engagement The latest annual planning cycle and the new structure I will apply The monthly performance review	Divide the business into manageable chunks Get the local leader to want to try another way – knock on the open door Create a local approach centred around Line Leader habits and coaching Create a review cycle with Intensity x Frequency	The employee engagement in that area changes The Line Leader grows HR is viewed differently I am viewed differently The senior leaders see a different way	Initial creation Daily and weekly work with the Line Leaders – coaching Get others to visit and see

It's **impossible** to engage somebody when **you're not engaged.**

The People Manager

In chapter one, we said the book was for three groups. In this chapter, we'll focus on the third group: The People Manager.

Who is The People Manager?

The People Manager is the Line Leader: the person the team reports to in the normal work capacity, i.e., the person you call your boss. They are the person who generally assesses your performance, manages your time and attendance, reviews your activity, approves your holidays and does your personal development review.

In most organisations, this is the person who is typically charged with engaging the team.
You might think they would be the obvious candidate; however, it depends on the organisation's maturity around the subject of Engagement. If engagement isn't clear-front and centre as that person's defined responsibility, then very often it is abandoned on the side-lines because the line leader's time is consumed by their own work; attending meetings and solving problems (the things only managers do). But whether individuals formally see themselves as engagement leaders or not, is irrelevant because they are.

Research shows people fall out of love with their boss before they fall out of love with the organisation. Anyone who has regularly carried out exit interviews will recognise the common reasons for leaving, such as feeling under-appreciated, a lack of support, or not being sufficiently challenged. These are all ultimately the job of The People Manager who is responsible for building the culture and leading the team.

Where would we find The People Manager? Imagine yourself sitting somewhere between the top and the bottom of the organisation, or in between the front line and the CEO, where everybody is a Middle Manager. Some people would say they're not: they would call themselves Senior Leaders, or Internal Organisation Directors, or Heads of Business, but fundamentally, they're all Middle Managers. And therefore, from an engagement point of view, they're all engagement leaders, because generally they're managing their team, or trying to.

Let's consider what it's typically like for this middle management group. There are a number of things that exist in the middle management conundrum. I'll walk you through them so that you've got a clear picture of what it's like to be in the boots of these individuals. I'm talking about this from the experience of sitting in their seats, as well as from meeting the people who sit in those seats in our consultancy work.

The number one obstacle that The Middle Manager has to deal with is that while they are formally responsible for engagement; there are three other informal engagement leaders who tend to float around them and who have a significant influence on their ability to engage.

The Three Influencers

The first influential leader is their boss. In my experience, most employees don't necessarily have a direct channel to their boss's boss, but they do see them and are impacted by them. They cast a shadow, which means the boss's boss impacts The People Manager's ability to engage.

Let's say I'm a Line Leader; my ability to engage would be heavily influenced by my boss. In my experience, there's an assumption that I'm engaged purely because I have the title of leader or manager. Our experience is that that's not true.

Lots of middle managers are disengaged. And that is an important point because what we've learned in our engagement consulting work while observing people in action, is that **it's impossible to engage somebody when you're not engaged. What's on the inside, eventually manifests itself on the outside.** As human beings, over millennia, we've learned to suss out authenticity, because historically, when we roamed the plains, our survival depended upon it. And now, in today's modern world, we still have that antenna.

If I'm not engaged as a Line Leader or People Manager, it's difficult to engage others, so the real question is; who creates the environment to engage the engager? And the answer is; their boss because they are on the boss's team.

Having spent years reflecting on this, and looking back to the Tom and Paul story from Chapter 1; as a group, in that environment, we viewed Paul as a bit of a 'brown-noser': somebody who sucked up to the boss. It took me a while to ask myself the question: What was Paul doing when he was sucking up to the boss?

As a team, we all knew and felt the shadow Paul was casting. Paul's boss, a guy called David, was an intelligent 'Tom'. He had the brains minus Tom's continual ranting. Looking back, I often ask myself: Was Paul sucking up to the boss for four hours a day, or was that his way of influencing the boss? Paul was operating in an environment where his boss probably wasn't big on engagement. If I had my time with him again, I'd ask Paul whether he was sucking up to the boss, or influencing the boss to try to make the business better?

One thing we knew for sure was, we weren't necessarily more engaged with the organisation, but we were engaged with Paul. And as a result, we were more engaged with the work he discharged on behalf of the business, so, Influencer Number One is the boss's boss.

Influencer Number Two for The Middle Manager to manage is their peer group. Time and again in our work, we come across leaders whose reason for not doing something, consciously or not, is the standard their peers set. Invariably where this is the case, we find that the leaders' teams look across to the next team and say things like, 'You want us to do something that they're not?' And it's as though the organisation has engagement paralysis based on the desire to maintain an order of fairness around equal effort to be disengaged. It's like they're sitting there saying, 'Let's all just be unhappy. If we're equal-ish around here, it'll be great.'

Therefore, the pressure of maintaining the norm is often greater than that of standing out. At the end of the day, we're pack animals, and rejection from the pack is painful and scary. Again, using Paul as an example... For some reason, Paul was okay with being a brown-noser, even though his fellow supervisors appeared not to be; he seemed fine on the fringes and he managed the grief that came with it.

So, the question for you, the reader, is:
What about you?
Where are you on the 'prepared to be different and stand out' scale?

Are you happy to except the risk of alienation by your peers? Or is it easier for you to fit in and live with mediocrity?

We've got the boss's boss, the peer group, and then there's Influencer Number Three, which is the team you lead. In the Tom and Paul story, there was an old fellow who put his arm around me and said, 'It's okay, son. They're management; they don't give a shit.' What if he'd said, 'Let's do this in spite of management?' or 'I'll tell you what. Let's team up and work together.'

And what if he had directed me down a path of engagement, irrespective of what management did, rather than directing me down a path of disengagement?

The idea that it's solely the job of the Line Leader to engage the team is fool's gold. It's an archaic view, of an organisational operating paradigm where the leader is the fulcrum of a team's success. My experience is that employees these days are just as powerful and intelligent as the leaders; they're just as well-educated and as influential.

It's a flawed paradigm to think it's only the responsibility of the leader to engage. Often the team know who is disengaged before the leader does; they see it every day, and they allow it to exist.

If you think about it; just at a basic human respect level, why would you allow your colleague to come into work every day and be bloody miserable, knowing they hate their job? And in the more extreme scenarios, why would you allow them to influence other colleagues to be disengaged? So, there's this third group which is just as influential as the leader. I'm not saying that it's not the responsibility of The People Manager to set the tone and cast the first shadow because there's no doubt it should be their primary goal to engage people on a daily basis. I'm not saying that these three influencers are the reason a Line Leader should abdicate responsibility, but I am saying it is more difficult for Line Leaders because of these three groups. It's even harder when you don't understand what's going on beneath the surface and why problems keep occurring.

A good example of what it looks like within the team context would be from when I worked at Toyota; we worked hard to recruit the right character into the business, and we had a good hit rate. But occasionally somebody would wriggle through the system and what you saw in the workplace was fascinating because in a very short space of time, what had previously been a harmonious team, quickly became discontented. You could feel and see it because the team would ostracise the disengaged person. In a short space of time, you'd spot the person with the wrong attitude sitting alone during the coffee break in the rest area. You'd hear the team say, 'That person's not pulling their weight.' And you'd even hear people say to the person, 'You need to buck your ideas up because you're letting us down.' And it would bubble up to the Line Leader; as a supervisor in that environment, I knew within ten weeks that I'd got a problem person who was disengaging the team. In that organisation, it was easy for me to remove the individual because our systems and processes were all aligned to achieve engagement. We never hesitated because the engagement of the team was more important to us than one person's job.

In the example of you being the Line Leader, those three groups of Influencers are really important. But then there's other stuff you would have to understand which happens within the Engagement space. The first factor is — let's say I worked my way up through the organisational structure from age sixteen, and I'm now fifty-one. During those thirty-five years, I've attended numerous management training courses, supervisor trainings, leadership courses. But in all of those years and training opportunities, I've never been offered one course on engagement. Nobody ever formally taught me about engagement. Nobody ever said, 'We're going to go on the engagement course now, Mark.' They frequently said, 'We're going to go on the supervisory leadership course,' which taught me how to problem-solve and manage project plans, and then someone from HR might teach me about the Grievance and Discipline Policies, and how to manage absences, but, no one ever taught me Engagement.

There are two reasons for this monumental oversight: One is, engagement wasn't a 'thing' back then — it wasn't mentioned at all in management talks and strategy. But even today, I'd be prepared to bet, if I went into a range of major organisations, they wouldn't have a Supervisory Engagement Leadership Course. They might have a paragraph in a Supervisory Leadership course, consisting of a few token hours. And I know this because it's what we see when we begin working with new clients, which means that leaders aren't even trying to engage — they are too focused on meeting their Key Performance Indicators (KPIs) or juggling surveys. With that in mind, why would we expect them to be good at engagement?

The second reason is that when you're in the middle manager's boots, depending on your organisation, there's either zero-engagement dialogue or in the other extreme, you're faced with countless Employee Opinion Surveys. There's a wide spectrum whereby some leaders never have an engagement conversation, and others have woken up to the need to engage and spend hundreds of thousands of pounds on surveys.

You may think this sounds like a positive development, but one of the many problems with Employee Opinion Surveys is that they contain defined dimensions which often sound good but are meaningless and impossible to quantify. An example would be where the survey asks about environmental factors, hygiene factors, your ability to talk to your leader, and the channels to express your voice. Feedback is submitted as verbatim comments which are worthless because they're anonymous, so you can't even follow up with the person who wrote them.

Most comments are relevant to something that's happened historically, or something that was frustrating at the moment they responded to the survey. Add to that, the average take-up on a survey is only about 40%, at best, and you can see why although I would have data, it's useless information. The icing on the cake is the manager then gets bombarded by requests to give a response to the data, which generally comes in the form of, 'What's your plan?' The typical overwhelmed People Manager would then try to create a plan based on this random data. If you're a People Manager, this will probably sound familiar!

Very few people believe that the Engagement Gantt Chart is of any value; it's generally requested by the boss, who merely responds to the organisation's routine expectations. If you say to most line leaders, 'Where's the response to the output of the Employee Opinion Survey on your to-do list?', you'd be lucky if it's in their top ten because that's not how results are measured, and so it's not a priority. I've been complicit in this survey merry-go-round, so I'm not saying I haven't made the same mistakes.

I've looked at opinion surveys and at graphs showing where I'm supposedly weak, and I made a plan, only to look at the plan twelve months later, to see that nothing had been achieved because nobody asked me to achieve it. I was asked to achieve the KPIs, and so naturally, that's what I focused on. In the meantime, I received a new Opinion Survey and made yet another plan which I didn't achieve, and so on... Only the Corporate Centre chased me because they had boxes to tick, and it's their job to police procedures. I doubt that even the Corporate Centre believe it's a productive exercise.

All of this was going on, while I was supposed to be engaging people, and they were looking at me thinking, **'There he goes again with another one of his meaningless plans. Why doesn't he just talk to us and ask us what we think?'** This hopeless scenario creates a common conundrum: you have a group of people making plans, based on fuzzy data, for no real purpose. That's what I call a waste of time!

The Middle Manager operates with these three groups of big influencers around them, are typically not trained in the principles of Engagement and they're either not asked for anything tangible to do with Engagement, or they are asked to make plans that will never be implemented, and nobody cares about or believes in. This is a reliable summation of what it's like to be a People Manager.

The Good News

I know first-hand what The People Manager's world is like and how you have to deal with all of this crap that you think is completely out of your control. The good news is that by focusing on some habits that are within your control, you'll start to role model a set of behaviours which won't just change and impact your team, but will also change what your boss, your peers and your team thinks. And as a bonus for adopting these simple Engagement Habits, it'll even change corporate's view of what's supposed to happen! Stay with me because we'll cover those habits in the next section.

> Focusing on some habits that are within your control, you'll start to role model a set of behaviours which won't just change and impact your team, but will also change what your boss, your peers and your team thinks.

If you live in a world where no one is serious about Engagement, **you're going to have to be brave.**

The Twelve Engagement Habits of The People Manager

In the previous chapter, we covered how The People Manager needs to role model some habits to engender high levels of engagement, and we will now review these habits.

Many of the habits apply to the things we spoke about in earlier chapters, regarding the CEO and the Centre, but we're now looking at them through a different lens.

As we look at the habits; I want you to remember three things:

1. These habits are only built on the foundation of trust that we discussed in Chapter Two. Therefore, when building the habits, you need The People Manager to focus on the high-trust way.
2. These habits are not independent of one another; the way to think of them is like individual strands and, when woven together, they create a tapestry of engaging leadership.

3. You have a choice. These habits are from mine and Alex's experience, and they work best when you use them to spark your thinking. We all need to create our own solutions (habit routines) because then they are naturally tailor-made for us.

Please bear in mind that these habits are not an exhaustive list of things you can do because there will be other things that occur to you when you're thinking creatively and open to new solutions. We've found that guiding people to create positive habits and to find their own answers is far more productive than telling people what they should or should not do – People Protect What They Build.

The Twelve Habits

Habit 1: Connect with the Influencers.

We covered the three groups of influencers within the engagement conversation: your boss, your peers and your team members. If you're going to be able to build engagement within the team, you need to create an umbrella of confidence for everything you do with these three groups. It's tough for those around you to support you on one thing if you're not delivering, or at least don't appear to be delivering, on others. Quite simply, you have to have credibility and reliability (or at least perceived credibility and reliability) in your job or role before people will allow you to present and run with new ideas. Remember the trust equation from Chapter Two.

There are various ways to create credibility and reliability where it's lacking, and the detail will be individual to your circumstances. Think of this as a habit routine — Cue: I have made a commitment; Routine: Irrespective of what I have to do personally I will deliver on that commitment; Reward: I get a credit in the credibility and reliability bank account. However, don't forget you must practice the habits based on a foundation of trust.

Doing An Edison.

Let's say you are seen as reliable and credible, and people are prepared to listen to you about this Engagement proposition.

In this case, you can do what I call an 'Edison'. Thomas Edison used to announce at a press conference and declare that he was going to invent something. And then he'd go and invent it. It's as simple as that. He used his show of commitment at the press conference as a way to drive himself to create what he'd declared he would invent.

This public commitment approach worked for me too; I would declare that I'm going to work on Engagement and that I wanted to do it with my team, and I would explain what it would look like, so they knew what to expect. I felt as though that gave me the license to begin moving in a new direction, and also to prepare people to follow once I'd figured out what we'd be doing.

Choosing Stealth.

Another way which is excellent if you haven't got the desired level of credibility and reliability is to choose stealth. You've probably noticed that things are generally only as big as you make them, so if you don't make a big deal of what you're doing, other people won't usually take it as a big deal. Then you can begin to work on Engagement by stealth, or under the radar.

Choose whichever way suits you, but both need to result in you connecting and involving the influencers at some point.

Habit 2: Be Brave.

If you live in a world where no one is serious about Engagement, you're going to have to be brave.
You have to develop the habit of putting Engagement first. Otherwise, it'll just drift into the background as it has in the past because the company will ask you to prioritise different things. Being brave requires you to put Engagement first on your agenda, and to manage the influencers, the organisation and the business, in

such a way that Engagement doesn't get side-lined again.

An example of this is, when I was a Middle Manager at Ford, I had some credibility and reliability, so I was able to do an Edison. I said I was going to establish what we would call a 'standard diary'. I told my teams that at a particular time of day, I would go and see them, so at say seven-thirty until eight o'clock every day, I would be with the same team.

At eight-fifteen until eight forty-five, I would be with another team. I created this schedule as a pictorial diary, and I told everyone what to expect, and then I followed through. You've got to follow through, or you'll lose your credibility and reliability! I did it this way because I wanted to carve out the time as well, which I'll talk more about in a different habit. Still, in creating the standard diary, I created a commitment to be with my teams at certain times, which gave me both the opportunity and the time to engage. I was transparent about my intention, which is a high trust behaviour.

It was all going great until about two weeks in when I was walking across the factory floor, and my boss's boss rang me. And he said he would like me to come to a meeting in his office at eight-thirty. To honour my Engagement commitment, I had to say that I couldn't come because I had an appointment with my team. As you may imagine, that didn't go down well at all, and he said he didn't care, and that meeting in his office was more important.

I knew all of my hard work would be wasted if I caved in to his demands, so I told him that although I understood his perspective, I must follow through on what I had already scheduled with the team. I suggested an alternate time to meet with him, and somehow, we managed to fumble through, and I breathed a sigh of relief. Until the next time it happened.

And then on the third occasion, my boss's boss, who was an authoritarian type, said something about ramming my standard diary up my backside if I didn't get to his office immediately! I took a deep breath and calmly replied that he would have to come down to the shop floor and find me, to do that.

If you commit to Engagement, you have to be brave when you're challenged – because you will be. I'm not saying the approach I took at Ford is the right one; I've always had a bit of a laissez-faire approach to authoritarian management, so I'm not recommending you do it my way if it's not your style. But you do have to figure out a way to be brave that's authentic for you.

Habit 3: Belief First.

In the 1980s, you may recall that we had public information films about not drinking and driving, and they had some impact. But then over time, the effect plateaued and tactics needed to be more sophisticated as we gained a greater understanding of human behaviour, and realised that the way to change behaviour is to focus on the thoughts and conditioning that predicate behaviour, rather than the behaviour itself. In our consultancy work, our good friend and colleague Michael Finnegan, calls it The Belief Tree. And, the behaviour that's manifested itself is a result of a set of feelings. Those feelings are a result of an attitude, and the attitude is a result of what we believe. And what we believe is the result of the way we become conditioned over time, to think a certain way.

What we've learned about psychology and the way we think about things is that if you want to change behaviour, first you've got to change your thinking. The campaign moved from 'Don't Drink and Drive', because it's naughty, to one of images of children being knocked over and killed because it is an emotional state which conditions our thinking. That conditioning created a belief in individuals that drinking and driving was wrong, and an attitude that anyone who did it was a social pariah. Now, instead of worrying about being caught by the police, most of us worry about the consequences of hitting a child or the attitude of friends and our community to those who may choose to pick up their car keys after a long night at the pub. The lesson for policy makers was not to 'tell people' not to do it, but to work on their beliefs, and as a result influence our attitudes and those around us. This habit is about spending time to understand the team's beliefs around engagement, rather than their behaviour.

Therefore, if you follow the metaphor of a tree, the roots of the tree are our conditioning and beliefs, or what we think is right and wrong. The trunk is our attitude, the branches are our feelings, and the leaves are our behaviours; the outward manifestation of what we do. If you think about that in organisational terms; when a business does an employee opinion survey, what they're predominately doing is talking about the leaves. They're trying to understand why the leaves are brown instead of investigating what the problem is in the roots.

To engage people in their work, and in your business goals, you need to discover what's driving their disengaged behaviour which stems from their belief system. People will question you and what you're doing, and if there's a history of failed attempts at creating change, they'll say they've tried it all before, and it doesn't work.

This is because they don't believe it will work with their current belief system. They're not saying the solution you're presenting them with today isn't workable; they're saying what their belief system thinks, which is why the high trust habit of listen first without agenda in order to understand is the place for the leader to start. Engagement is the outcome of that effort, rather than the result of 'trying' to engage people.

Habit 4: Connect the Compass to the Map.

It's essential to connect the compass to the map continually. We covered the CEO's role in Chapter Two, we spoke about the CEO creating the direction, and we described it as a compass. This habit is about allowing people to draw their own map. We often come across leaders who talk about how difficult it is to connect employees with the direction of the business: the vision, where they're going and their strategy. When I hear this, I ask them a simple question, which is, 'How often do you talk to people about the vision?' The typical reply is that they don't talk about it often, although they are more than happy to tell people what they should do next (i.e. their map). They might mention it at the start of a meeting, and at a quarterly business review but the connectivity of the compass to the map, doesn't occur through a brochure or a poster on the wall. It manifests through the everyday actions of leaders, how much they share it with their teams, and how effective they are at connecting with their people as they share the vision.

Remember one of our earlier principles was that People Protect What They Build, and for this reason, you've got to allow them to build. What we have found is there are three common scenarios:

1. There's a business where the boss hasn't defined or shared the vision.
2. There's a boss who has defined the vision, and filled in the detail to such an extent that we can't really get involved.
3. It's the perfect situation where the boss has provided a compass, and there's enough opportunity to create the connection.

If you're in scenario number one or two, the best way to view it is that you now have an excellent opportunity to have a conversation with the team about how to make the vision come alive. You've got the chance to talk to the influencers about what the detail means in practical terms, and you can get them involved in the conversation which is exactly what you want.

If you're in scenario number three with the optimum solution, you've got the compass without the map, and you start talking to the team and building the daily habit of asking them for their input and encouraging them to get involved. The starting point we advise is for The People Manager to ask a few simple questions: What does it mean to you? How does this relate to your work? These are the details that the map needs for individual teams.

A couple of other things to bear in mind when you're working with the team to build this habit is to ask them to talk about the past, the present and the future. Many businesses declare visions that only talk about the future; not many reflect on the past, which is unhelpful because it's the past, not the future that stops most people from taking action. When you want somebody to make a move, logic and emotion have to be in balance; If they're out of kilter, people hesitate. Most businesses fire off logical reasons at people about why we must change because of our quality rating, safety performance or customer satisfaction scores. While it makes logical sense, it doesn't transform people's behaviour unless emotion and logic are aligned, and you talk about the vision daily.

An example I often use is when I was at Toyota, and I had a Japanese boss. Each day he would walk around the shop floor and the offices, and I began to notice that every time he saw me, he would take the opportunity to talk to me about my work.

He would ask what I was up to and how it was going, and he would listen. Once he'd listened to me, he would find a way to connect what I'd said to the company vision. He would talk about the business priorities and how they connected to the work I'd just been describing, and he would emphasise how it fed into the greater scheme of things, which made me feel appreciated and recognised.

This is where the continual connection of the compass and the map comes into play because you've got to help people draw the map and then find a way to keep it central to the conversation.

In our consulting work, we talk to leaders about what we call the Buzz Lightyear Effect. Most research on the subject of communication will say you've got to continue to communicate, and it may be as much as seven to ten times to get your message across, but what we've found from experience that the real number is infinity. There isn't a single silver bullet; you've got to keep talking about it, and this is what creates the Buzz Lightyear Effect: communicate to infinity and beyond!.

The ultimate thing for The People Manager to remember is that the vision is about your people so you must help them to see, touch and feel how the vision will tangibly work for them. If you don't help them do that, it's going to be challenging to engage them in the objectives of the business.

Habit 5: Create a Personal Connection.

I ask some questions when I talk to a People Manager so I can get a good understanding of the business. The first question would be, 'Do you have the disposition to empathise, sympathise, and support the people you have an emotional connection with?' And the second question is, 'Would you go the extra mile for those you care about most?' When you ask a People Manager these questions, they typically answer yes.

The third question would be, 'How well do you know your team, and how well do they know you?' The answers vary but lean towards, 'Not that well.'

If you imagine positioning these questions on both sides of a weighing scale, the scale is usually out of balance. And in my experience, it's because there's a belief that there should be a gap between the boss and the people; otherwise what would happen when you have to give them bad news? There's an assumption that if you're too close, you won't be able to do it effectively. I think it's nonsense, and that knowing your people well means you understand them better and when it's necessary, you can deliver bad news in a kinder, more personal way. I don't buy into the old-school, keeping your people at arms-length mentality, and it doesn't work well for building engagement. When the scales are balanced, it's easier to engage people because they want to listen to you, and you are keen for each other to succeed. Toyota is the best I've seen at creating this balance. I lost count of the number of times I went the extra mile at Toyota because I felt guilty about letting someone down; be it the team, my boss, or the organisation. On numerous occasions, I left work and jumped into the car, key in the ignition, and then realised I couldn't leave without finishing something. And it was never because my boss pressured me, but always because of the emotional connection I had with the team and the business.

What I've found is that when I ask a leader how many people work for them, they might say fifty or one hundred, but if you ask how many people report directly to them, the answer is invariably no more than ten. And then when I probe further and ask if they can name the partners of the ten people, I discover they usually can't. They don't know if they have children, or what their hobbies are. It's a barometer of how well the leader is connected with their people and shows a lack of understanding and rapport.

If you are in a similar position, a good starting place to build this habit is to begin showing interest in your team and asking those questions. Many people will happily share, but some won't, and that's okay too; they will know you made an effort.

Creating a personal connection and balancing the scales is critical for Engagement.

Habit 6: Don't Give Fantasy Oxygen.

Fundamentally; in the absence of fact, people create fantasy. Human brains are brilliant at creating images; we join the dots, and if we haven't got sufficient dots, we find a way to connect them up and create an image from our imagination. I come across business leaders who decide to create a barrier around what's going on; company updates are stifled and evasive, especially in times of change. And when leaders retreat into silence, it's typically because they think it's better to say nothing than to disrupt people.

Leaders get stuck in the fear that there has to be perfect communication, which is a misnomer because there is no such thing. Perfection is only ever in the ear of the receiver. Communicate frequently, otherwise, people will make up their own story which is potentially more harmful than the truth. Courageous conversations may be required, and of course, you can't betray confidences, but you must stay true to the principle of maintaining Engagement rather than trying to control the news. It's preferable to be honest and to say that you've been explicitly told not to share information because it's sensitive, rather than avoiding the issue.

When there's a company restructure with possible redundancies on the horizon or anything problematic within the business, leaders need to face the issues head-on or the situation will grow worse, and People Managers then find themselves in engagement quicksand. People make up their own 'truths', and when this occurs, it's like fantasy oxygen which burns like napalm; rumours spread quicker than factual news.

Our experience is that the real reason most businesses stay silent is they are fearful of the unknown; they are terrified of how employees, the Legal and HR departments will react.

Scenario

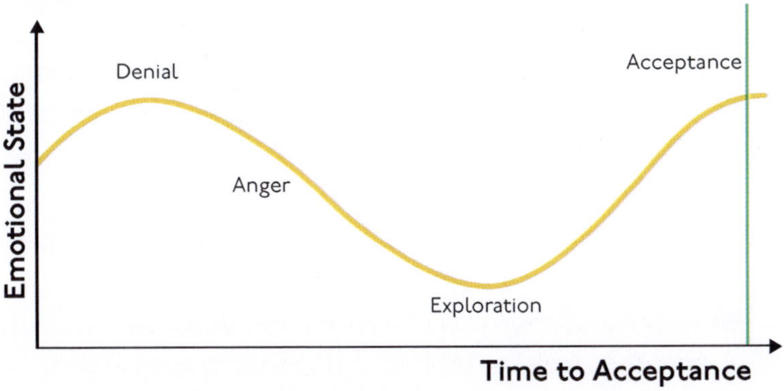

The curve (The Kubler-Ross Curve) shows how people go through four stages when they're managing an emotional state based on something negative they've heard. There's denial, anger, exploration and acceptance.

What generally happens in businesses is there's a timeline of when something needs to be communicated, and to happen, which is indicated by the green line on the graph.

Typical scenario

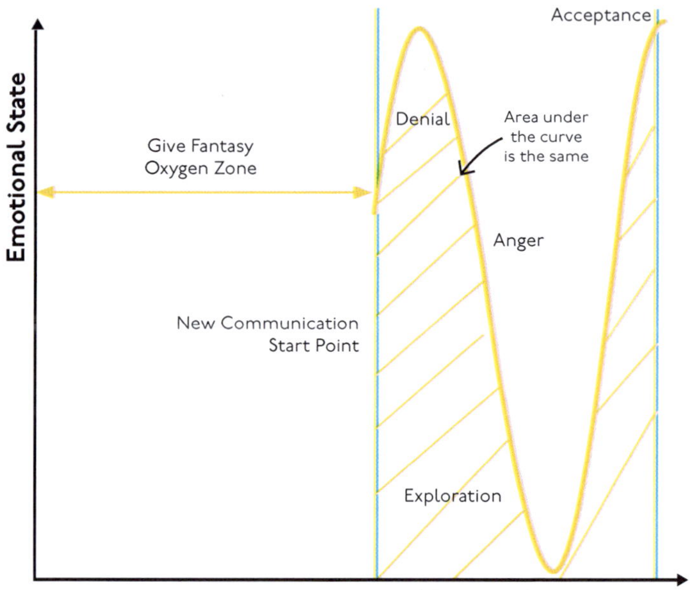

This is the point at which people have to accept whatever is about to happen, but what businesses don't realise is that if you say nothing, they reduce the available time for people to reach acceptance, which means cramming the change curve into a shorter time, so the peak of it is higher, and the trough of it is deeper. The area beneath the curve doesn't change, so people still need to go through the curve, which will be more difficult in a shorter time. And when you say nothing, you create what we call the fantasy zone because people will know something is going on.

Speaking openly, often and with as much passion as you can muster, allows employees to draw their own conclusions, with less anxiety, so they reach acceptance quicker, and in a calm rather than an exhausted state of mind.

Habit 7: Make Time to Engage.

When I was a Line Leader, I seemed to spend all my time trying to deliver what others wanted, such as business initiatives, boss and team demands. I had no time to focus on what I wanted, which was to engage people. I was so busy being busy that I lost sight of it, and then one day when I was reflecting, I realised I was going about it all wrong because I knew how to create time but I wasn't applying my knowledge to the concept of Engagement. If you'd told me to create time to solve a production problem, I would have done it, and so the real question became, why was I not creating the time to solve the Engagement problem? The habit, therefore, was to put Engagement first, figure out where it went in my schedule and then stick to it. **Everything changed when I created time for it.**

Have you noticed that your boss rarely gives you something to do and also takes something away to balance up your workload? As a result, I started to ask myself what I needed to take off my to-do list to give me time to create Engagement. But then I realised that while I needed some specific times where I focused on Engagement in my schedule; everything I did was an engagement opportunity. I used to say, and still say today in my own company, that every time we open our mouths, we create culture, and we must be mindful of what we say. And it's the same with engagement opportunities; every time you do something, you have an engagement opportunity, so I stopped thinking of it as separate to our daily business, and I recommend you do the same.

In terms of focussing and locking Engagement into the schedule, there are various models like in the Standard Diary example I referred to earlier. And Covey's 'Seven Habits of Highly Effective People', help us to prioritise the important over the urgent.

You must get into the habit of putting Engagement first, sticking to your schedule, and seeing everything you do as an engagement opportunity. As in the example of my boss who talked to me on the shop floor, it only took two minutes to connect the work I did with the company vision, which was him integrating Engagement into his job.

Habit 8: Become Comfortable with Difficult Conversations.

You need to develop a habit of being comfortable with difficult conversations because a leader's desire to engage in a meaningful way is directly proportional to the number of difficult conversations they have. Successful relationships in the workplace, and all areas of life, are fraught with conflict. I don't mean war-like conflict: When you use the word 'conflict', people tend to think about arguments, but by conflict, I don't mean it's necessarily a bad thing.

Some people have a conflict, and the way they manage it is to avoid an argument, and they choose to smile and walk away. The conflict hasn't been resolved, but it's non-confrontational. And while it might seem that not rocking the boat is the best way to create a smooth-sailing organisation, my experience is you can't break negative patterns and achieve growth without rocking the boat and risking getting wet. It's often during a disagreement that Engagement is created, therefore always agreeing does not necessarily equal an engaged team.

To create Engagement, you have to have challenging conversations. Leaders often have conversations collectively with everybody in the team, or they only talk to people individually, but they need to do both. Over the years, discussions about Employee Engagement have become more mainstream, and the opinion is prevalent that to improve Engagement and encourage happiness, leaders should reduce the focus on performance, which frankly I think is rubbish.

Our experience shows that challenge of individual and team performance is a primary motivating factor which drives Engagement. You only have to Google it, and you'll find surveys by Gallup and Harvard Business Review to back it up; it's well known that managing performance positively creates Engagement.

In our consultancy work, the way we do this is to help leaders focus on what we call **The Performance Curve.**

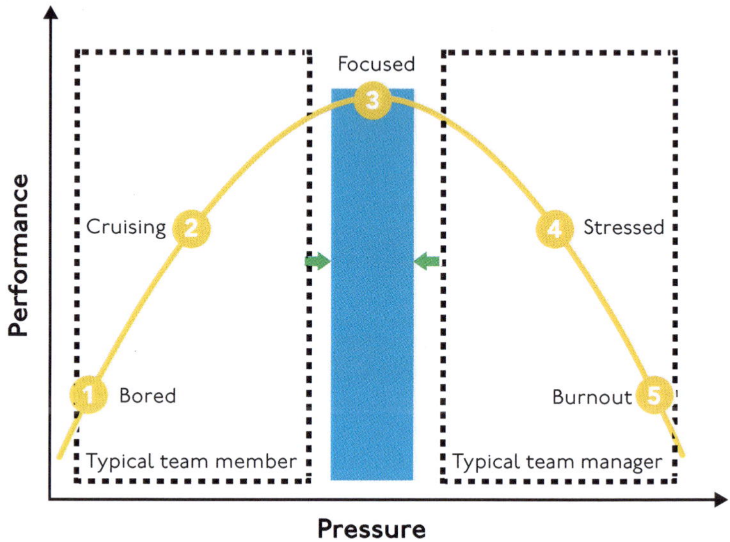

In the Engage for Success research, they described engaging managers as people who focus their people, giving them scope, treating them as individuals, coaching and stretching them. To do this effectively, you have to be willing to create opportunities for uncomfortable conversations. A company full of yes and no people is a stale one with low engagement. Let me give you an example of a conversation I hear in a lot of teams, in many organisations all over the world. Imagine a local team meeting to discuss the day's or the week's performance and priorities. The team gather weekly, the team leader chairs the discussion and tends to stand or sit at the front, and does the majority of the talking, with contributions from most of the team. However, person X is there! You can feel their disinterest and see it in their body language. If asked to contribute it is clearly a chore, and an interruption to what is to them, another boring, pointless day. The meeting concludes and we move on to the next meeting to repeat the cycle. Where was the challenge from the leader or the team members? When we ask most leaders this question, the typical answer is rooted in the desire to avoid conflict.

In this case, person X is saying 'no', and the leader and the team are accepting that no, which seems crazy, right? So, what's the current habit routine that the leader is role modelling, and what should it be? Person X isn't just disengaged; they are creating leader and team disengagement and it is being accepted! However, the reality is it is ultimately the leader who has to have the habit of challenging this through a difficult conversation in order to reposition person X on the performance curve.

Habit 9: Respond with Lightning Speed.

In many management teams, there's an underlying belief that the key to engagement is to obtain succinct briefs. While this may be helpful, I don't believe teams need more telling what to do. The Samaritans have a beautiful little ethos: 'We don't just hear, we listen.' Listening is only the start because after listening and hearing, you've also got to be able to respond quickly.

We've probably all experienced a leader saying to

leave it with them, or even worse, giving a politician's answer which is not to respond at all. These examples are the antithesis of what creates engagement because high engagement requires the leader to speak openly and to respond with lightning speed. And responding with lightning speed doesn't mean just giving any old response, it means giving a considered response. Even if the response is to say that you don't have the answer but you will get back to them. The key difference is in you meaning it and actually getting back to them. When people receive an evasive response or none at all, over time, they stop contributing because there's nothing in it for them. This results in team members saying there's no point as it goes nowhere.

Time and again, I've sat with senior leaders and line managers, listening to them talk about what they can and can't say because they think saying the 'wrong thing' will give the wrong impression and come back to haunt them in the future; they pursue the perfect answer. As there isn't such a thing as a perfect answer because it always depends on how the words are received; not having the perfect answer can serve as a powerful conversation starter, provided you enjoy difficult conversations! When you don't know the answer, or don't have all the details, just be open and honest. We have found that responding with lightning speed is difficult in large organisations where generating a considered response may rely on other people, and for that reason, it might feel as though it's out of your control. In this situation, you have to organise yourself to find a way to respond because if you don't, you'll be up against the fantasy oxygen problem.

An excellent example of this is in our work with one of our large blue-chip clients. In the beginning, the speedy response was not their strong point, so we created a mechanism to manage the process, which consisted of a group who would meet weekly and answer employees' questions. By the way, if you are thinking that weekly isn't that quick, remember this was for 'them'!

If an employee provided their name, we gave it a personal response; if not, we included the response in the weekly newsletter. Initially, we had an avalanche of questions, but it soon settled down to a steady flow. The secondary impact was that leaders became faster responders as they noticed the benefits.

Habit 10: Don't Assume You Understand the Emotional Backpack.

When you start to work on engagement, you learn that everybody has an emotional backpack. The skill of an engaging leader is to keep the backpack light. If I ask you about a previous employer, you'd probably share something that was in your emotional backpack which you didn't like about them. It's also important

> Don't assume you understand the Emotional Backpack

to note that we carry this emotional backpack everywhere, and so if it's not well managed, it will take a toll on the engagement proposition.

Leaders often remark that they understand something because they used to do a particular job. They assume they know what it's like now. I explain to them that just because that is their autobiography, doesn't mean they understand because they're not in the other person's shoes.

A good friend was talking to me about their sixteen year old and how they couldn't get them to understand something. I observed how much the world has moved on since we were the same age. It was clear to me that he assumed that he still knew what it was like to be a sixteen-year-old even though thirty years had passed.

A lot of people managers, specifically if they've come up through the ranks, hold the assumption that when they did a job, it must be the same as it is now. They think they understand what's in someone's emotional backpack, which isn't helpful.

This awareness, combined with practising the other habits, will result in lighter backpacks all round.

Habit 11: Recognise the Hierarchy of Needs.

If you're not familiar with this concept, Google 'Maslow's Hierarchy of Needs'. Everyone in your organisation sits somewhere in that hierarchy, and if they're in the low echelons on the hierarchy, don't expect to gain traction in Engagement. In Maslow's terms, there is Physiological, Safety, Belonging, Esteem, and Self-actualisation. Physiological is about having sufficient food, water and air. Safety is concerned with security, law and order, rules, limits and regulations. If employees worry about those two areas, you will be wasting your time trying to engage them in anything.

People need the basics covered to be able to flourish. An example of this is when I worked with the regional management team of a well-known high street pharmacy chain. There was a team of fifty people across the British Isles, and the programme was about Engaging Leadership. We asked to speak to some of the workers in the stores, and we started talking about leadership. One person said, 'Don't talk to me about leadership; come and look at this!' And they led us to the rest area at the back of the store where they showed us mushrooms growing near the toilets. I could talk about Engagement until I was blue in the face, but sometimes you just need to get rid of the mushrooms.

I delivered a conference speech, and at the end of it, somebody came over to me and asked whether I could help them with a problem. They told me that their company was struggling and every time they tried to talk to the employees, all they ever wanted to talk about was the air-conditioning in the restroom because it was too warm. They asked me what I thought they should do. I said, 'Fix the air-conditioning in the restroom.' Sometimes it is that simple.

There is no point talking about Employee Engagement before you've got the basics right. As a People Manager, trying to lead and engage people in a poor environment, is difficult, so first of all, get into the habit of recognising employee concerns and not just brushing them aside because otherwise, they weigh down a person's backpack. When broken air-conditioning units and mushrooms in the toilets are in someone's backpack, they will be slow moving.

Think about what it would take to get rid of the mushrooms. In this case, it was just a Stanley Knife, some weed killer and not using the toilet for eight hours. If you can't get the air-conditioning unit fixed immediately, you could buy a couple of fans and explain to the team that it's a temporary solution. At the same time, you work on getting the air-conditioning unit fixed. Figure out what's in your control and what's not, and that way, you can find and implement solutions.

Habit 12: Getting the Right Team.

This is a simple proposition with two principles, both of which are critical to building Engagement. The first principle is what I call The Bouncer Principle. I had an interesting conversation with a doorman bouncer where he explained that people believe bouncing is about brute force and having the ability to grab people by the scruff of the neck and boot them out. I was intrigued and asked him to tell me more. He said that there are good and bad bouncers and that he likes to think he's a good one. He went on to explain that a good bouncer can identify the people who are going to cause trouble, and therefore not let them in. He worked on the concept that if you think they're going to be a problem, don't let them in, and it struck me that so often in business we knowingly let people in even though we suspect they will be a problem. The real trick isn't to know how to kick them out, but not to let them in at all. As a People Manager, you have to get into the habit of being clear who you want to allow in.

You might think you've got no control over the process because you don't interview everybody. Still, when you practice these habits, you will have a lot more influence with the stakeholders, your peers and your boss, so it becomes easy to help them to decide who to let in. Who you let through the front door impacts employee engagement. If people are challenging to work with and create tension in the team, they might not pull their weight, and as a result, these characters switch off the rest of the team. They're like poison, which leads us to the second principle: remove the bad apples. This is nothing new, but it's critical for Engagement. If you've got a barrel of good apples and you drop one bad one in, over time the whole barrel of apples turns rotten, conversely, if you've got a barrel full of bad apples, and you put one good apple in, unfortunately, the good apple doesn't turn all the rotten ones into good apples. Use The Bouncer Principle to not let bad apples in, but if they slip through, you have to remove them. You will probably add some bad apples: people who poison the rest of the team, so you have to get into the habit of managing the performance of the bad apples because if you allow them to continue to underperform, you'll struggle to create Engagement.

Example People Manager habit
Habit 5: Create a personal connection

1: The Current Paradigm	2: Cue	3: Routine	4: Reward	5: Focused Practice
What's going to stop me building the new habit?	What will trigger the new habit loop I want?	What is the pathway I wish to follow?	What will make me do it again?	When and how?
Time – it takes time to have a conversation, time I don't have I might have to share things I don't want to	A scheduled slot in my diary to think about this week's conversations The weekly team meeting	Twice a week I will have a conversation with two members of the team that is not work related It will take 5 mins I will record key facts of interest: family, hobbies etc for future conversations	The desire to make this natural The feeling I get the next time I do it The response I get from the team members	Twice weekly at the end or start of some other conversation

Example People Manager habit
Habit 8: Become comfortable with difficult conversations

1: The Current Paradigm	2: Cue	3: Routine	4: Reward	5: Focused Practice
What's going to stop me building the new habit?	What will trigger the new habit loop I want?	What is the pathway I wish to follow?	What will make me do it again?	When and how?
The conflict that might ensue The energy it will take The harmony of the team I don't get paid for this grief	The recognition that a team member is not in the focused zone A request from another team member Team and individual performance not where it needs to be	Create the environment to challenge the issue Do it quickly i.e. with an hour of its recognition Be transparent with respect to the issue Listen first Ensure I clarify the expectation, including how things will change or next steps	The change in performance The response from the team The feeling that I am building engagement irrespective of how it might feel in the moment	Within an hour of occurrence

To help people like us who have spent a lot of their career **screaming on the inside.**

Final Words

As you're reading this final chapter, it means one of two things: You're curious and can't wait to see what happens at the end, or our preferred version of events; you've been so inspired by the insights in this book that we've been able to hold your attention until the end.

Hopefully, you've already started building new engagement habits and are having different conversations across your organisation.

Here's a quick recap of the key points from the previous chapters:

- The key to engagement is building and embedding the right habits across the distinct organisational groups: From the top; the CEO. From the front line; the people leaders. And from the supporting functions; typically, HR or employee engagement.
- Engagement habits are easy to understand but require hard work to build, as they require consistent, focused purposeful practice with intensity and frequency. But now you know what these habits look like.
- Habits are just routines with a Cue, a Routine, and a Reward. All you have to do is figure out this sequence of events in the context of your situation, environment, or organisation.

And don't forget, it is handy to understand if there is anything that may stop you from starting or that may interrupt your habit building. We call this your 'Current Paradigm'.

If these practical insights resonate, remember you're building a set of habits, which means one habit, alone, while making a difference, will not be the silver engagement bullet. Building even one new habit can be challenging, but building a set is often a continual internal struggle, so, don't be too hard on yourself and expect immediate perfection. It will take time, but I promise you it is worth the effort.

As we have gone through this book, we've provided a few examples of habit loops, and we have provided a blank copy of the Proforma for you, which is the little matrix we use in our consulting work with our clients.

However, if you have got to this point and you are still not inspired to implement the insights in this book, the reality is that you're probably not going to do anything, and our advice would be to finally be honest with yourself. Change jobs and admit that leading people is not what you want to do. It's okay, but please allow someone to fill the engagement void, as the job and business will never get better if you're unwilling to make changes. It will always be a daily struggle and an annual battle of wills which is a terrible waste of talent and potential within the organisation.

Final Words

1: The Current Paradigm	2: Cue	3: Routine	4: Reward	5: Focused Practice
What's going to stop me building the new habit?	What will trigger the new habit loop I want?	What is the pathway I wish to follow?	What will make me do it again?	When and how?

The Final Word.

While we said at the start of this book we will not make a case for why you need Engagement, and we haven't; it's worth remembering that building employee engagement is not wholly altruistic. There is a definitive business benefit, and the evidence and the case for it is now so strong that it's undeniable. Whether it is safety, quality, productivity, customer service, customer loyalty, sales, revenue, defect rate, whatever measure you use, all of these are intrinsically connected at their root by one thing:

Engagement. If in doubt and you still want to be convinced then just Google it. You'll find reams of research to back it up.

However, for us, the real intent of this book was to help people like us who have spent a lot of their career screaming on the inside as they attempt to navigate what at first appears to be a hopeless merry-go-round of engagement, and we hope we have done that!

The Final, Final Word . . .

Don't forget, engagement needs engagement habits. **No habits = no engagement.** If you are happy to sit on the plateau of performance mediocrity, go ahead. However, if you want more, you now know what to do.

Love,

Mark and Alex

Mark & Alex would like to thank a few unsung heroines and heroes:

Anne Gregory – for her unwavering love and support

Fam Gregory – Ella, Siobhán, Orla, Rory, Cara & Sinéad for keeping me entertained

Jo Lewis – My rock during an itinerant career

Rhys Lewis – The wisdom behind my toughest decisions

Rachel Henke – for her word magic!

The Definition Team – for making it pretty

Greig Walker & John Kilner – for screaming with us

People are often **unreasonable, illogical** and **self centered**; ***Forgive them anyway.***

If you are kind, people may accuse you of selfish, ulterior motives; ***Be kind anyway.***

If you are successful, you will win some false friends and some true enemies; ***Succeed anyway.***

If you are honest and frank, people may cheat you; ***Be honest and frank anyway.***

What you spend years building, someone could destroy overnight; ***Build anyway.***

If you find serenity and happiness, they may be jealous; ***Be happy anyway.***

The good you do today, people will often forget tomorrow; ***Do good anyway.***

Give the world the best you have, and it may never be enough; ***Give the world the best you've got anyway.***

You see, in the final analysis, it is between you and your God; ***It was never between you and them anyway.***

Mother Teresa

Printed in Great Britain
by Amazon

23794612R00082